RUDOLF STEINER (1861–1925) called his spiritual philosophy 'anthroposophy', meaning 'wisdom of the human being'. As a highly developed seer, he based his work on direct knowledge and perception of spiritual dimensions. He initiated a modern and universal 'science of spirit', accessible to anyone willing to exercise clear and unprejudiced thinking.

From his spiritual investigations Steiner provided suggestions for the renewal of many activities, including education (both general and special), agriculture, medicine, economics, architecture, science, philosophy, religion and the arts. Today there are thousands of schools, clinics, farms and other organizations involved in practical work based on his principles. His many published works feature his research into the spiritual nature of the human being, the evolution of the world and humanity, and methods of personal development. Steiner wrote some 30 books and delivered over 6000 lectures across Europe. In 1924 he founded the General Anthroposophical Society, which today has branches throughout the world.

THE THREE WISE MEN AND THE BIRTH OF JESUS

RUDOLF STEINER

Compiled and introduced by Margaret Jonas

RUDOLF STEINER PRESS

Rudolf Steiner Press,
Hillside House, The Square
Forest Row, RH18 5ES

www.rudolfsteinerpress.com

Published by Rudolf Steiner Press 2017

Bible quotations are all taken from the Revised Standard Version (with the exception of quotations within the previously published lectures)

A catalogue record for this book is available from the British Library

Print book ISBN: 978 1 85584 537 4
Ebook ISBN: 978 1 85584 497 1

Cover by Morgan Creative featuring the Three Magi, St. Apollinare Nuovo, Ravenna
Typeset by DP Photosetting, Neath, West Glamorgan
Printed and bound by 4Edge Ltd., Essex

Contents

PART ONE

The Birth of Jesus 3
1. Karlsruhe, 12 October 1911 11
2. Basel, 18 September 1909 22
3. Basel, 19 September 1909 25
4. Bern, 6 September 1910 33

PART TWO

The Magi and their Teaching 39
5. Basel, 23 December 1920 44
6. Berlin, 19 January 1911 50

The Star of the Magi and their Gifts 59
7. Bern, 6 September 1910 62
8. Berlin, 30 December 1904 64
9. Cologne, 25 December 1907 70

PART THREE

Who Were the Three Magi? 77
10. Munich, 7 December 1909 82
11. Budapest, 31 May 1909 86

What Became of the Three Wise Men? 88
12a. Esoteric Lesson, possibly Karlsruhe, 21 or 23 January 1911 92

From Conversations with Rudolf Steiner 104

12b. Notes from personal conversations with Rudolf Steiner regarding the Master Jesus and Christian Rosenkreutz 105

Sources of Extracts 108

Notes 109

Editor's note: The spelling of Persian names in English varies considerably. Rudolf Steiner often appears to have used the version 'Ahura Mazdao' for the Zoroastrian deity. However, 'Ahura Mazda' is the spelling more commonly found in translations of Zoroastrian scriptures and works on the religion.

PART ONE

The Birth of Jesus

Now when Jesus was born in Bethlehem of Judea in the days of Herod the king, behold, wise men from the East came to Jerusalem, saying, 'Where is he who has been born king of the Jews? For we have seen his star in the East, and have come to worship him.'

When Herod the king heard this, he was troubled, and all Jerusalem with him; and assembling all the chief priests and scribes of the people, he inquired of them where the Christ was to be born. They told him, 'In Bethlehem of Judea; for so it is written by the prophet:

"And you, O Bethlehem, in the land of Judah are by no means least among the rulers of Judah; for from you shall come a ruler who will govern my people Israel."'

Then Herod summoned the wise men secretly and ascertained from them what time the star appeared; and he sent them to Bethlehem, saying, 'Go and search diligently for the child, and when you have found him bring me word, that I too may come and worship him.' When they had heard the king they went their way; and lo, the star which they had seen in the East went before them, till it came to rest over the place where the child was. When they saw the star, they rejoiced exceedingly with great joy; and going into the house they saw the child with Mary his mother, and they fell down and worshipped him. Then, opening their treasures, they offered him gifts: gold and frankincense and myrrh. And being warned in a dream not to return to Herod, they departed to their own country by another way.

(Matthew 2:1–12)

These words begin a story that will be familiar to many, whether from hearing the reading or from images on Christmas cards or school nativity plays and will evoke all kinds of feelings from joy to sorrow and doubt; but the enquiring reader will note that the proclamation of the birth to shepherds does not appear here, but is in St Luke's account (Luke 2:1–20). The reader may then note other apparent discrepancies—the Wise Men's visit takes place in a *house* (verse 11) and in Luke's account the birth takes place in a stable—a more familiar image. Only in Luke's version is there the story of Mary's cousin Elizabeth giving birth to John the Baptist six months earlier. But the main difference, often overlooked, will be in the two differing genealogical tables, briefly put—'Joseph' in Matthew's Gospel descends from King David's son Solomon, and in Luke's Gospel 'Joseph' descends from David's other son, Nathan. This is never satisfactorily explained by theologians—'mistakes' or 'intentions to show Mary's descent' carry little weight—unless we are prepared to accept an explanation that at first appears more startling and even improbable, but which nevertheless has some backing from ancient prophecies, hidden gospels and other more obscure material. Thanks to Rudolf Steiner's remarkable penetrating gifts of spiritual research, he was able to lay before his listeners the idea that the evangelists are describing *two different births*—two infants, both named Jesus, born to two sets of parents, both Mary and Joseph (common names at that time), in Bethlehem in Judea, but not at exactly the same wintertime. This would explain why Luke's Jesus is born to parents who have travelled from Nazareth in Galilee for purposes of census and tax but who return to their home some time afterwards, via Jerusalem for the presentation of Jesus in the temple, quite peacefully and in no apparent danger, while in Matthew's story the Wise Men's visit unwittingly unleashes a terrible massacre by the jealous King Herod of all baby boys under two years old—Joseph being warned by an angel to remove his family to safety in Egypt just in time. To describe the chronology of these events is beyond the scope of this study—readers are recommended to look at the book *The Time of Christ*, by Ormond Edwards[1], in which the detailed explanation unravels many discrepancies by looking at the different calendar systems in use in those days.

Steiner's explanation moreover opens up a mighty spiritual panorama of two births long prepared and of two very different individuals—the one in Matthew's Gospel being of an old soul with many incarnations behind him, who has accrued much spiritual wisdom. This child, we learn, was the reborn Zarathustra (or Zoroaster), who founded the Zoroastrian religion and guided the ancient Iranian peoples in their early mission around 6000 BC, but who was known of better in a later incarnation in the sixth century BC as Zaratas or Nazaratos—more of this will be considered in Part Two. The Jesus child of St Luke was entirely different—we have to be prepared to accept the idea of an 'unfallen soul'—an aspect of 'Adam' before the Fall as described in the Bible, held back and preserved and not incarnating in a human body (though working spiritually through others) until the birth as described. This child into whom, moreover, the astral forces of the Buddha worked was all *love* and without 'original sin', i.e. it had not been separated (sundered) from the Godhead. It may be hard today to imagine such a being. Steiner's explanation becomes even more remarkable when we learn how the two families came together as neighbours living in Nazareth. At the age of twelve, Jesus as described by

Luke, goes with his parents to the temple in Jerusalem as they did every year at the Passover, but this time a strange event occurs. His parents start on their return journey and then realize Jesus is not with the party—many others would have been travelling also—including the other family. On returning to Jerusalem they discover Jesus in the temple speaking in a most wise and knowledgeable way with the priests and rabbis. It was quite uncharacteristic for this normally dreamy, gentle boy to engage in theological conversation of this kind. Rudolf Steiner describes that at this point, the ego—or 'I' individuality of the Matthew boy, i.e. Zarathustra's—had left that body and passed into the body of the Luke boy, who henceforth became a remarkable individuality combining great wisdom with the greatest heart forces, until the mighty event of the Baptism, 18 years later, when the Christ Being descends into these carefully prepared sheaths and the Zarathustra ego leaves. After the temple experience at the age of twelve, the boy from whom the ego withdrew died soon afterwards. Steiner makes the comment that this kind of transference is not as rare as we might imagine and could explain many otherwise inexplicable human puzzles.

One can find the mystery of the two Jesus children veiled in many paintings of the Renaissance masters.[2] The temple event just described is shown by Ambrogio Borgognone, *The Children in the Temple*. Here are two boys, dressed alike in a similar coloured robe. Jesus as one sits in the centre, speaking to the learned priests at his left side—but he is looking at the other boy in the forefront, like himself, haloed, but paler, who is presumably being led away by his mother. Art historians refer to the custom of showing consecutive scenes in one painting, but here it is clearly all one scene and the sad pallor of the boy in the forefront is in contrast to the radiant Jesus boy in the centre. Many 'childhood of Jesus' paintings show two little boys—the second is usually taken as being John the Baptist, and indeed he is often painted draped with a hairy skin to indicate John's camelhair garment—and sometimes even historians consider that John's attributes were probably added later by another artist. However, there exist paintings with *three* boys, such as the beautiful *Madonna del Duca di Terranuova* by Raphael. John, in a hairy garment, stands on Mary's right, looking at Jesus on her lap while to her left stands another little haloed boy.

Regarding paintings, moreover, the great masters always distinguished between the two nativity stories, although as time went on, artists began to combine them. Paintings showing the visit of the shepherds usually show Jesus either in the manger or lying on the ground, the ox and the ass looking on,[3] as the shepherds arrive. In the nativities with the Wise Men, Jesus is normally shown seated on Mary's lap, upright and alert, frequently blessing the kneeling 'kings'. Secrets, whether wholly or partly understood, were handed down, quietly, by master to pupil for fear of accusations of heresy. If any early Christians were also aware of this secret knowledge, it was successfully purged together with most of the Gnostic teachings from the fourth century onwards.[4] A few references have survived however. In the fourth extract which follows, Steiner makes reference to the Gospel of the Egyptians.[5] This can be found in *The Apocryphal New Testament*[6] and is worded as follows:

> iii.13.92. When Salome inquired when the things concerning which she asked should be known, the Lord said: When ye have trampled on the garment of shame, and when the two become one and the male with the female is neither male nor female . . .

> (The so-called Second Epistle of Clement has this, in a slightly different form, c.xii.2:
>
> For the Lord himself being asked by someone when his kingdom should come, said: When the two shall be one, and the outside (that which is without) as the inside (that which is within), and the male with the female neither male nor female.)

Another mysterious account which would seem to be describing the merging of the two Jesus boys is described in the surviving Gnostic text, the *Pistis Sophia*:[7]

> Mary answered and said... When thou wast little, before the Spirit came upon thee, the Spirit came from the height whilst thou wast in a vineyard with Joseph, and came unto me in mine house in thy likeness, and I knew it not, and I thought that it was thou. And the Spirit said unto me: Where is Jesus my brother, that I may meet with him? And when it spake thus unto me, I was in perplexity, and thought that it was a phantom come to tempt me. I took it therefore and bound it to the foot of the bed that was in mine house, until I should go forth unto thee and Joseph in the field and find you in the vineyard, where Joseph was staking the vineyard. It came to pass then, that when thou heardest me tell the matter unto Joseph, thou understoodest the matter, and did rejoice, and say: Where is he, that I may behold him? Otherwise I will tarry for him in this place. And it came to pass, when Joseph heard thee speak these words, he was troubled: and we went together and entered into the house and found the Spirit bound to the bed. And we looked upon thee and upon it, and found that thou wert like unto him: and he that was bound to the bed was

> loosed, and embraced thee and kissed thee and thou also kissedst him and ye became one.

The Essenes, the strict esoteric Jewish sect to which the Nazareth families seem to have had some connection, also had their ancient prophecies relating to the coming of *two* Messiahs—one priestly and one kingly. A descendant of Solomon would be seen as kingly, and that of Nathan, priestly. The Dead Sea Scrolls discovered at Qumran in the 1940s and '50s are now known to have been Essene texts; scholars have noted the references to two Messiahs, one stemming from the House of David—'prince of Israel'—and the other from that of Aaron, the first high priest, to whom the kingly Messiah must defer. And indeed the ego of the 'Solomon' child renounces his body and own bloodline to enter into that of the 'Nathan' child. Geza Vermes writes:[8]

> As befits a priestly sect, however, the Priest-Messiah comes first in the order of precedence; he is also called the 'Messiah of Aaron', the 'Priest', the 'Interpreter of the Law' . . . The King-Messiah was to defer to him and to the priestly authority in general in all legal matters . . . The 'Messiah of Aaron' was to be the final Teacher, 'he who shall teach righteousness at the end of days'.

And the Messianic Rule text goes as follows:

> When God engenders (the Priest-) Messiah, he shall come with them at the head of the whole congregation of Israel with all his brethren, the sons of Aaron the Priests . . . and then the Messiah of Israel shall come, and the chiefs of the clans of Israel shall sit before him . . . And when they shall gather for the common table, to eat and to drink new wine . . . let no man extend his hand over

> the firstfruits of bread and wine before the Priest; for it is he who shall bless the firstfruits of bread and wine, and shall be the first to extend his hand over the bread. Thereafter, the Messiah of Israel shall extend his hand over the bread . . .

There is also a rather better known prophecy in the Old Testament which can be read as relating to *two*: 'A star shall come forth out of Jacob and a sceptre shall rise out of Israel . . .' (Num. 24:17).

Although a full discussion is not within the scope of this work, we must also point out that the term 'Virgin birth' as traditionally taught by the churches is a misunderstanding. For instance, Rudolf Steiner makes this comment:

> 'And she who gave birth to this Being was filled with the power of the Spirit of the Universe'—If we feel the sanctity of such a Mystery we shall realize that in this way of presenting it there is something infinitely higher than any of the exoteric interpretations of the Virgin Birth . . . one point is this: Why should the writer of St Matthew's Gospel have enumerated the whole sequence of generations from Abraham to Joseph if he had wished to indicate that the birth of Jesus of Nazareth had no connection with this line of descent? He is at pains to show how the blood was led down the generations from Abraham to Joseph; how, then, could he possibly have intended to indicate that the blood of Jesus had nothing to do with this blood?[9]

Readers are referred to Emil Bock's book *The Childhood of Jesus*[10] where this mystery is more fully explored.

Margaret Jonas, August 2017

1. Karlsruhe, 12 October 1911

We know [from former lectures] that in Palestine, at the time which concerns us, not one but two Jesus children were born, one of them from the Solomon line of the House of David. This is the Jesus child of whom the Matthew Gospel speaks. The peculiar contradiction between the beginnings of the Matthew and the Luke Gospels derives from the fact that the writer of the Matthew Gospel was concerned with one of the Jesus children, the one born from the Solomon line. Then, at almost but not quite the same time, another Jesus child was born, from the Nathan line of the House of David.

The important thing is to understand clearly what kind of beings these two children were. Occult investigation shows that the individuality who was in the Solomon Jesus child was none other than Zarathustra. After Zarathustra's most important mission, of which we have spoken in connection with the ancient Persian civilization, he had been incarnated again and again—lastly during the Babylonian-Chaldean civilization, and now as the Solomon Jesus child. This Zarathustra individuality, with all the great and powerful inner forces which in the nature of things he had brought over from earlier incarnations, had to incarnate in a body descended from the Solomon side of the House of David, a body adapted for working up and further developing the great faculties of Zarathustra in the way that human faculties, when they are already at a very high level, can be brought further on in so far as they belong to the being who is going from incarnation to incarnation. We are concerned therefore with a human body which did not wait until later years to work on these faculties, but could do so in a youthful, childlike and yet powerful organism. Hence we see the Zarathustra-individuality growing up in such a way that the faculties of the child developed comparatively early. The child soon showed an extent of knowledge which would normally have been impossible at his age.

One fact, however, we must keep firmly in mind: the Solomon Jesus child, although the incarnation of so lofty an individuality, was only a highly developed man. Hence he was encumbered—as even the most highly developed man must be—with certain liabilities to error and moral difficulties, though not exactly vices or sins. Then we know that in his twelfth year the individuality of Zarathustra, by an occult process known to everyone who has made himself conversant with such facts, forsook the body of the Solomon Jesus child and went over into the body of the Nathan Jesus child. Now the body of this Nathan Jesus child—or, better, his threefold bodily organization: physical body, etheric body, astral body—was formed in a quite special manner. In fact, this body was such that the child showed capacities exactly contrary to those of the Solomon Jesus child. Whereas the latter was remarkable because of his great gift in relation to things one can learn externally, it might almost be said that in this respect the Nathan Jesus child was untalented. You will understand that saying this implies not the slightest deprecation. The Nathan Jesus child was not in a position to familiarize himself with the products of human culture on earth. By contrast, the remarkable fact is that he could speak as soon as he was born. A faculty which belongs more to the physical body was thus present in him from his birth. But—according to a good tradition which can be occultly confirmed—the language he spoke could be understood by his mother only. The child's most strongly marked characteristics were qualities of the heart. He had an immense capacity for love and a disposition capable of immense self-sacrifice. And the remarkable thing is that from the first days of his life his mere presence, or his touch, had beneficent effects—magnetic effects, one might perhaps call them nowadays. Thus all the qualities of heart were manifest in this child, enhanced to such a degree that they could have a beneficent magnetic influence on his environment.

We know also that active in the astral body of this child were the forces which had once been acquired by that Bodhisattva who became Gautama Buddha. We know indeed—and in this respect the oriental tradition is absolutely correct, for it can be confirmed by occult science—that the Bodhisattva, who on becoming the Buddha five centuries before our era no longer needed to incarnate further on earth, worked from the spiritual world upon all those who devoted themselves to his teachings. It is characteristic of such an individuality, who rises to heights from which he need no longer incarnate in a body of flesh, that he can then take part in the affairs and destiny of our earth existence from out of the spiritual worlds. This can happen in the most manifold ways. In fact, the Bodhisattva who went through his last incarnation on the earth as Gautama Buddha has taken an essential part in the further evolution of humanity. Our human spiritual world stands continually in connection with all the rest of the spiritual world. The human being not only eats and drinks and so takes into himself the substance of the physical earth; he continually receives soul-spiritual nourishment from the spiritual world. In the most varied ways forces continually flow into physical earthly-existence from out of the spiritual world. Such an inflow of the forces which

Buddha had gained for himself came into the wider stream of humanity through the fact that the Buddha forces permeated the astral body of the Nathan Jesus child. We know, too, from earlier lectures that the words we still have today as a Christmas message—'The Divine reveals itself from the heights, and on earth peace will spread in the hearts of men of good will!'—originate in essence from the influence which flowed down into human evolution through the immersion of the Buddha powers in the astral body of the Nathan Jesus child . . .

Today the most important thing for us is to establish that in the astral body of the Jesus child described by Luke we have the Buddha forces at work. And when this Nathan Jesus child was twelve years old, the Zarathustra individuality passed over into his threefold being.

Why is it, then, that this Jesus child had the remarkable qualities we have just characterized? It was because he was not a human individuality like every other, but in a certain respect quite different, and in order to understand him we must go back to the ancient Lemurian time in which, strictly speaking, the Earth evolution of man took its start. We must clearly understand that everything before the Lemurian time was really only a repetition of the Saturn, Sun and Moon periods. Only in the Lemurian time was the first germ-condition laid down in man as a potentiality, so that during the Earth evolution he could receive the fourth member of his being, the ego. We can say the extension of mankind over the earth—a subject dealt with more precisely in the *Outline of Occult Science*[11]—is to be traced to certain human ancestors in the Lemurian period, the period with which our present earth took its start.

It is only after a certain point of time in this Lemurian

period that we can speak correctly, in a modern sense, of the human race. Before this, those egos who have since continued to incarnate were not present in men on earth. They were not yet separate from the substance of that hierarchy which had first brought the human ego into being: the hierarchy of the Spirits of Form.[12] We can now picture to ourselves—occult research shows this—that part of the substance of the Spirits of Form entered into the incarnations of men for the building up of the human ego. But when in due time man was given over to his physical incarnations on the earth something was held back. A certain ego substance was not brought into the stream of physical incarnations. If we were to represent the stream of physical human incarnations, beginning with him whom the Bible calls 'Adam', the progenitor of the human race, we should have to draw a genealogical tree with widespreading branches. Instead, let us simply imagine that the substance poured down from the Spirits of Form now flows onwards, but that something was held back: an ego that was now protected from entering into physical incarnations. Instead, this ego preserved the form, the substantiality, which man had had before proceeding to his first earthly incarnation. This ego lived on collaterally with the rest of humanity, and at the time of which we are now speaking, when the Event of Palestine was to take place, it was still in the same condition, if we wish to speak according to the Bible, as was the ego of Adam before his first embodiment in flesh.

In examining what occult science knows about this ego—which naturally for modern man is something extremely foolish—we see that this ego, which was, as it were, held back 'in reserve', was given into the care of the Holy Mysteries through Atlantean and post-Atlantean times. It was preserved in an important Mystery centre, as in a tabernacle, and because of this it had quite special characteristics; it was untouched by everything that a human ego could have learnt on earth. It was therefore untouched by any luciferic and ahrimanic influences; it was indeed something we can think of, in contrast to other human egos, as an empty sphere, still completely virginal with regard to all earth experiences—a nothing, a negative, in this respect. Hence it seemed as though the Nathan child, described in the Luke Gospel, really had no ego; as though he consisted only of physical, etheric and astral body. And it is quite adequate if at first we say that an ego, developed as egos had developed in Atlantean and post-Atlantean times, was not there at all in the Luke Jesus child.

We speak in the true sense of the words when we say that in the Matthew Jesus child we have to do with a complete human being, whereas in the Nathan Jesus child of the Luke Gospel we have to do with a physical, an etheric and an astral body which are interrelated in the harmonious unity that belonged to man when he emerged from the Saturn, Sun and Moon evolutions. Hence this Jesus child, as the Akashic Record[13] tells us, was untalented for all that human culture had developed. He could not receive it because he had never been among it. External abilities and adaptations to existence are the outcome of certain experiences in earlier incarnations. Anyone who had never shared in such experiences would show himself without talent for all that people have accomplished during the earth evolution. If the Nathan Jesus child had been born in our time, he would have been totally ungifted for learning to write, since in Adamic times writing was unknown. By contrast, the Luke Jesus child revealed in a high degree the qualities he had brought with him—qualities that had not fallen into decadence through the luciferic influence. Even more interesting is the remarkable language he spoke . . .

. . . The languages which are now spread over the earth took their rise comparatively late in evolution: they were preceded by what can truly be called a primal human language. It is the disuniting spirits of the luciferic and ahrimanic world who have made many languages out of the primal language. The primal language is lost, and can be spoken today by nobody with an ego which in the course of earth evolution has passed from incarnation to incarnation. This Jesus child, who had not gone through human incarnations, acquired from the starting point of human evolution the faculty of speaking, not this or that language, but a language of which we can rightly say that it was not comprehensible to those around him. But, because of the inner qualities of heart that lived in it, it was understood by his mother's heart. This points to a phenomenon of immense significance in the case of the Luke Jesus child.

We have seen that when this Luke Jesus child was born he was provided with everything that had not been influenced by the lucifer-ahrimanic forces. He did not possess an ego that had been through a series of incarnations; therefore nothing had to be discarded when, in his twelfth year, the individuality of Zarathustra passed over from the Solomon Jesus child into the Nathan Jesus child. I have already said that the human element which had remained behind, and up to this time had developed in the mysteries by the side of the rest of humanity, was born for the first time in the Palestine period as the Nathan Jesus child. There was a transference from a mystery centre in Western Asia,[14] where this human kernel had been preserved, into the body of the Nathan Jesus child.

This child grew on, and in his twelfth year the individuality of Zarathustra passed into him. We know also that this passing over is intimated in the scene of the twelve-year-old Jesus in the Temple. It was quite natural that the parents of the Nathan Jesus child, who were accustomed to regard him in the light we have described, should find a remarkable change when they discovered him in the Temple after he had been lost. For that was the moment when Zarathustra passed over into this twelve-year-old child. From the twelfth to the thirtieth year, therefore, we have to do with the individuality of Zarathustra in the Luke Jesus child.

Now in the Luke Gospel we have a remarkable expression which indicates something that can be made clear only by occult investigation. You know that in the Luke Gospel, after the description of the scene with the twelve-year-old Jesus in the Temple, there is a passage: 'And Jesus increased in wisdom and stature, and in favour with God and man' (Luke 2:52). In truth this passage stands as follows when we restore the text of the Gospels from the Akashic Record. The twelve-year-old child increased in everything wherein an astral body can increase, i.e. in wisdom; in everything wherein an etheric body can increase, i.e. in all the qualities of kindliness, goodness, etc; and in everything wherein a physical body can increase, i.e. in all that pours itself into external beauty of form. In this passage, therefore, a special indication is given that the Jesus child, not having gone from incarnation to incarnation, had up to his twelfth year remained untouched, and could not be touched in his individuality, by the luciferic and ahrimanic forces. The Luke Gospel intimates this again by tracing the sequence of generations back through Adam to God, thus indicating that the substance in question was uninfluenced by all that had taken place in human evolution.

So this Jesus child lived on, increasing in all that was possible for a threefold organism not touched by the contamination which has affected the threefold bodies of other human beings. And this enabled the individuality of Zarathustra, from the twelfth to the thirtieth year of life, to pour into this threefold human being all that could come from the heights to which he himself had previously attained. Hence we form a correct idea of Jesus of Nazareth, up to the thirtieth year of his life, when we think of him as a lofty human individuality, for whose coming into existence the greatest possible preparation had been made.

But we must now be clear about one thing if we want to understand how the fruits of a development we go through in our bodies are of benefit to the individuality. Our bodies enable our individuality to absorb the fruits of our life for its future evolution. When in death we forsake our bodies, we do not usually leave in them what we have achieved and gained for ourselves as individuals. Later on we shall see under what special conditions something may remain in the bodies; but it is not the rule that the individuality should leave behind in his bodies whatever he has won for himself. When Zarathustra forsook the threefold bodily being of Jesus of Nazareth in the thirtieth year, he left behind the three bodies: physical, etheric and astral. But all that he had been able to gain through these instruments went into the individuality of Zarathustra and lived on further with him, to his benefit. Something, however, was gained by the threefold bodily organism of Jesus of Nazareth. His human nature, still free, as it always had been, from luciferic and ahrimanic influences, was conjoined for a period with the individuality who had unequalled insight into the spirituality of the cosmos.

Think what this Zarathustra had experienced! While he

was founding the ancient Persian civilization and looking up to the great Sun Spirit, he was even then gazing out into the cosmic realms of the spiritual. Through successive incarnations his development went on. When the innermost part of human nature, together with the most intensive powers of sympathy and love, had become manifest through the unsullied human substance which had been preserved until the birth of the Nathan Jesus, and when the astral body had permeated itself with the forces of Gautama Buddha, there was present in this child what we may call the most intimate inwardness of man. And then into this bodily nature there entered the individuality who above all others had seen most clearly and deeply into the spirituality of the macrocosm. By this means the bodily instrument, the entire organism, of the Nathan Jesus was so transformed that it could be the vehicle capable of receiving into itself the Christ-extract of the macrocosm. If this bodily nature had not been permeated by the Zarathustra-individuality up to the thirtieth year, the eyes would not have been able to endure the substance of the Christ from the thirtieth year up to the Mystery of Golgotha; the hands would not have been capable of being permeated with the substance of the Christ in the thirtieth year. To be able to receive the Christ, this bodily nature had to be prepared, expanded, through the individuality of Zarathustra. Thus in Jesus of Nazareth, as he was at the moment when Zarathustra took leave of him and the Christ-individuality entered into him, we have to do neither with an adept nor with anything like a higher human being. For an adept is an adept because he has a highly developed individuality, and it was just this that had passed out of the threefold bodily nature of Jesus of Nazareth. We have simply the bodily nature so prepared through the indwelling of Zarathustra that it could take into itself the Christ-individuality. But now, through the union of the Christ-individuality with this bodily nature, by necessity the following consequence came about.

During these three years from the Baptism by John in Jordan onwards to the Mystery of Golgotha, the development of the physical body, the etheric body and the astral body was quite different from the bodily development of other human beings. Since the Nathan Jesus had received no influence from the luciferic and ahrimanic powers, the possibility was given that, from the Baptism in Jordan onwards—now that there was in Jesus of Nazareth no human ego, but solely the Christ-individuality—everything which is normally at work in a human organism was not developed.

2. *Basel, 18 September 1909*

We now know who was born in Bethlehem when Joseph and Mary travelled thither from Nazareth, and we know whose coming had been announced to the shepherds; but that is not all. Much that is strange and significant took place at the beginning of our era in order to bring about the greatest Event in the evolution of humanity. For a better understanding of what gradually led up to that Event, we must still consider the following.

In the ancient Hebrew people there was a line of generations descending from David. We learn from the Bible that David had two sons, Solomon and Nathan. Thus two lines of descent, the 'Solomon line' and the 'Nathan line' stemmed from David. Leaving aside the intermediate members, we can say: At the beginning of our era, descendants both of the Solomon line and of the Nathan line of the House of David were living in Palestine. In Nazareth there lived a man named 'Joseph', a descendant of the Nathan line; he had a wife, 'Mary'. And in Bethlehem there lived a descendant of the Solomon line, also named 'Joseph'. It is not in the least surprising that there were two men of David's lineage named Joseph and that each was married to a Mary as the Bible says. Thus at the beginning of our era there were two couples in Palestine, both bearing the names of 'Joseph' and 'Mary'. The Bethlehem couple traced back its origin to the 'Solomon' or kingly line of the House of David, and the other (the Nazareth couple) to the 'Nathan' or priestly line. To this latter couple (of the Nathan line) was born the child described to you... This child provided an astral sheath that could eventually be absorbed into the Nirmanakaya of the Buddha.[15] At the time when the child was due to be born, this couple of the Nathan lineage journeyed from Nazareth to Bethlehem—as St Luke relates—'to be taxed'. The genealogical table is given in his Gospel.

The other couple did not originally reside in Nazareth but in Bethlehem; this is related by the writer of the Gospel of St Matthew. This couple of the Solomon line also had a child named 'Jesus'. In the body of this child too a great individuality was living, but the child had a different task to fulfil. The wisdom of the world is indeed profound! It was not the function of this child to impart fresh forces of youth to the astral sheath; his mission was to bring to humanity that which only a *mature* soul can bring. Under the guidance of all the Powers concerned, this child was able to be the reincarnation of the individuality who had once taught the mysteries of Ahura Mazda to people in ancient Persia, who had once given up his astral body to Hermes and his etheric body to Moses, and who had appeared again as Zarathas or Nazarathos, the great teacher of Pythagoras in ancient Chaldea. This individuality was none other than Zarathustra. The ego of Zarathustra was reincarnated in the child of whom the Gospel of St Matthew relates that he was born of a couple named Joseph and Mary who descended from the kingly or Solomon line of the House of David and resided, originally, in Bethlehem.

Thus we find one part of the truth presented in the Gospel of St Matthew and the other part in that of St Luke. Both accounts must be taken literally, for truth is complex. We know now who was born from the priestly line of the House of David. But we know too that from the kingly line there was born the individuality who had once worked in ancient Persia as Zarathustra and had inaugurated the 'kingly' or 'magic' science of the ancient Persian kingdom. Thus the two individualities lived side by side: the young Adam-individuality in the child of the priestly line of the House of David, and the Zarathustra-individuality in the child of the kingly line.

3. *Basel, 19 September 1909*

The births of the two Jesus children were separated by a period of a few months. But Jesus of the Gospel of St Luke and John the Baptist were both born too late to have been victims of the so-called 'massacre of the innocents'. Has the thought never struck you that those who read about the Bethlehem massacre must ask themselves: How could there have been a John? But the facts can be substantiated in all respects. The Jesus of St Matthew's Gospel was taken to Egypt by his parents, and John, supposedly, was born shortly before or about the same time. According to the usual view, John remained in Palestine, but in that case he would certainly have been a victim of Herod's murderous deed. You see how necessary it is to devote serious thought to these things; for if all the children of two years old and younger were actually put to death at that time, John would have been one of them. But this riddle will become intelligible if, in the light of the facts disclosed by the Akashic Chronicle, you realize that the events related in the Gospels of St Luke and St Matthew did *not* take place at the same time. The Nathan Jesus was born *after* the Bethlehem massacre; so too was John. Although the interval was only a matter of months, it was long enough to make these facts possible.

You will also learn to understand the Jesus of the Gospel of St Matthew in the light of the more intimate facts. In this boy was reincarnated the Zarathustra-individuality, from whom the people of ancient Persia had once received the teaching concerning Ahura Mazda, the great Sun Being. We know that this Sun Being must be regarded as the soul and spirit of the external, physical sun. Hence Zarathustra was able to say: 'Behold not only the radiance of the physical sun; behold, too, the mighty Being who sends down His spiritual blessings as the physical sun sends down its beneficent light and warmth!'—*Ahura Mazda*, later called the Christ—it was He whom Zarathustra proclaimed to the people of Persia, but not yet as a Being who had sojourned on the earth. Pointing to the sun, Zarathustra could only say: 'There is His habitation; He is gradually drawing near and one day He will live in a body on the Earth!' . . .

Through his ego too, such an individuality is destined to fulfil a great mission. The ego of Zarathustra incarnated again and again in other personalities, for an individuality of such advanced development can always consecrate an astral body and strengthen an etheric body for his own use, even when he has relinquished his original bodies to others. Thus six hundred years before our era, Zarathustra was born again in ancient Chaldea as Zarathas or Nazarathos, who became the teacher of the Chaldean mystery schools; he was also the teacher of Pythagoras and again acquired profound insight into the phenomena of the outer world.

If we steep ourselves in the wisdom of the Chaldeans with the help, not of anthropology but of anthroposophy, an inkling will dawn in us of what Zarathustra, as Zarathas or Nazarathos, taught in the mystery schools of ancient Chaldea. The whole of his teaching, as we have heard, was given with the aim of bringing about concord and harmony in the outer world. His mission also included the art of organizing empires and institutions in keeping with the progress of humanity and with order in the social life. Hence those who were his pupils might rightly be called not only great 'magi', great 'initiates', but also 'kings', that is to say, men versed in the art of establishing social order in the external world.

Deep and fervent attachment to the individuality (not the personality) of Zarathustra prevailed in the mystery schools of Chaldea. These Wise Men of the East felt that they were intimately connected with their great leader. They saw in him the 'Star of Humanity', for 'Zoroaster' (Zarathustra) means 'Golden Star', or 'Star of Splendour'. They saw in him a reflection of the sun itself. And with their profound wisdom they could not fail to know when their master was born again in Bethlehem. Led by their 'Star', they brought as offerings to him the outer symbols for the most precious gift he had been able to bestow upon people. This most precious gift was knowledge of the outer world, of the mysteries of the cosmos received into the human astral body in thinking, feeling and willing; hence the pupils of Zarathustra strove to impregnate these soul-forces with the wisdom that can be drawn from the deep foundations of the divine-spiritual world. Symbols for this knowledge—which can be acquired by mastering the secrets of the outer world—were gold, frankincense and myrrh: gold, the symbol of thinking; frankincense, the symbol of the piety which pervades man as feeling; and myrrh, the symbol of the power of will. Thus by appearing before their master when he was born again in Bethlehem the Magi gave evidence of their union with him. The writer of the Gospel of St Matthew relates what is literally true when he describes how the Wise Men among whom Zarathustra had once worked knew that he had reappeared among humanity, and how they expressed their connection with him through the three symbols of gold, frankincense and myrrh—the symbols for the precious gift he had bestowed upon them.

The need now was that Zarathustra, as Jesus of the Solomon line of the House of David, should be able to work with all possible power in order to give again to people, in a rejuvenated form, everything he had already given in earlier times. For this purpose he had to gather together and concentrate all the power he had ever possessed. Hence he could not be born in a body from the priestly line of the House of David but only in one from the kingly line. In this way the Gospel of St Matthew indicates the connection of the kingly name in ancient Persia with the ancestry of the child in whom Zarathustra was incarnated.

Indications of these happenings are also contained in ancient books of wisdom originating in the Near East. Whoever really understands these books of wisdom reads them differently from those who are ignorant of the facts and therefore confuse everything. In the Old Testament there are, for instance, two prophecies: one in the apocryphal Books of Enoch pointing more to the Nathan Messiah of the priestly line, and the other in the Psalms referring to the Messiah of the kingly line. Every detail in the Scriptures harmonizes with the facts that can be ascertained from the Akashic Chronicle....

Thus we see two Jesus children growing up. The son of Joseph and Mary of the Nathan line was born of a *young* mother (in Hebrew the word 'Alma' would have been used), for a soul of such a nature must necessarily be born of a very young mother. After their return from Bethlehem this couple continued to live in Nazareth with their son. They had no other children; the mother was to be the mother of this Jesus only. When Joseph and Mary of the Solomon line returned with their son from Egypt, they settled in Nazareth and, as related in the Gospel of St Mark, had several more children: Simon, Judas, Joseph, James and two sisters (Mark 6:3).

The Jesus child who bore within him the individuality of Zarathustra unfolded with extraordinary rapidity powers that will inevitably be present when such a mighty ego is working in a body. The nature of the individuality in the body of the Nathan Jesus was altogether different, the most important factor there being the Nirmanakaya of the Buddha overshadowing this child. Hence, when the parents had returned from Bethlehem, the child is said to have been full of wisdom—that is, in his etheric body; he was 'filled with wisdom and the grace of God was upon him' (Luke 2:40). But he grew up in such a way that the ordinary human qualities connected with understanding and knowledge of the external world developed in him exceedingly slowly. A superficial observer would have called this child comparatively backward—if account had been taken only of his intellectual capacities. But instead there developed in him the power streaming from the overshadowing Nirmanakaya of the Buddha. He unfolded a depth of inwardness comparable with nothing of the kind in the world, a power of feeling that had an extraordinary effect upon everyone around him. Thus in the Nathan Jesus we see a being with infinite depths of feeling, and in the Solomon Jesus an individuality of exceptional maturity, having profound understanding of the world.

Words of great significance had been spoken to the mother of the Nathan Jesus, the child of deep feeling. When Simeon[16] stood before the newborn child and beheld above him the radiance of the being he had been unable to see in India as the Buddha, he foretold the momentous events that were now to take place; but he spoke also of the 'sword that would pierce the mother's heart'. These words too refer to something we shall endeavour to understand.

The parents were in friendly relationship and the children

grew up as near neighbours until they were about twelve years old. When the Nathan Jesus reached this age his parents went to Jerusalem 'after the custom', to take part in the Feast of the Passover, and the child went with them, as was usual. We now find in the Gospel of St Luke the mysterious narrative of the twelve-year-old Jesus in the Temple. As the parents were returning from the Feast they suddenly missed the boy; failing to find him among the company of travellers they turned back again and found him in the Temple conversing with the learned doctors, all of whom were astonished at his wisdom.

What had happened? We will enquire of the imperishable Akashic Chronicle.

The facts of existence are by no means simple. What had happened on this occasion may also happen in a different way elsewhere in the world. At a certain stage of development some individuality may need conditions differing from those that were present at the beginning of his life. Hence it repeatedly happens that someone lives to a certain age and then suddenly falls into a state of deathlike unconsciousness. A transformation takes place: his own ego leaves him and another ego passes into his bodily constitution. Such a change occurs in other cases too; it is a phenomenon known to every occultist. In the case of the twelve-year-old Jesus, the following happened. The Zarathustra-ego, which had lived hitherto in the body of the Jesus belonging to the kingly or Solomon line of the House of David in order to reach the highest level of his epoch, left that body and passed into the body of the Nathan Jesus who then appeared as one transformed. His parents did not recognize him; nor did they understand his words, for now the Zarathustra-ego was speaking out of the Nathan Jesus. This was the time when the

Nirmanakaya of the Buddha united with the cast-off astral sheath and when the Zarathustra-ego passed into him. This child, now so changed that his parents did not know what to make of him, was taken home with them.

Not long afterwards the mother of the Nathan Jesus died, so that the child into whom the Zarathustra-ego had now passed was orphaned on the mother's side. As we shall see, the fact that the mother died and the child was left an orphan is especially significant. Nor could the child of the Solomon line continue to live under ordinary conditions when the Zarathustra-ego had gone out of him. Joseph of the Solomon line had already died, and the mother of the child who had once been the Solomon Jesus, together with her children James, Joseph, Simon, Judas and the two daughters, were taken into the house of the Nathan Joseph; so that Zarathustra (now in the body of the Nathan Jesus child) was again living in the family (with the exception of the father) in which he had incarnated. In this way the two families were combined into one, and the mother of the brothers and sisters—as we may call them, for in respect of the ego they were brothers and sisters—lived in the house of Joseph of the Nathan line with the Jesus whose native town (in the bodily sense) was Nazareth.

Here we see the actual fusion of Buddhism and Zoroastrianism. For the body now harbouring the mature ego-soul of Zarathustra had been able to assimilate everything that resulted from the union of the Nirmanakaya of Buddha with the discarded astral sheath. Thus the individuality now growing up as 'Jesus of Nazareth' bore within him the ego of Zarathustra irradiated and pervaded by the spiritual power of the rejuvenated Nirmanakaya of the Buddha. In this sense Buddhism and Zoroastrianism united in the soul of Jesus of Nazareth.

When Joseph of the Nathan line also died, comparatively soon, the Zarathustra-child was in very fact an orphan and felt himself as such. He was not the being he appeared to be according to his bodily descent: in respect of the spirit he was the reborn Zarathustra; in respect of bodily descent the father was Joseph of the Nathan line and the external world could have no other view. St Luke relates it and we must take his words exactly:

> Now when all the people were baptized, it came to pass that Jesus also being baptized, and praying, the heaven was opened and the Holy Ghost descended in a bodily shape like a dove upon him and a voice came from heaven which said, Thou art my beloved Son, this day have I begotten Thee. And Jesus himself, when he began to teach, was about thirty years of age . . .

and now it is not said simply that he was a 'son' of Joseph, but: 'being *as was supposed* the son of Joseph' (Luke 3:21–3)—for the ego had originally incarnated in the Solomon Jesus and was therefore not connected fundamentally with the Nathan Joseph.

4. *Bern, 6 September 1910*

Thus two streams became one. There was now *one* Being. In the Gospel our attention is specially called to the following. Not only did the parents notice a startling change, detecting something they could not possibly have expected, but this change also showed itself outwardly. When the boy Jesus had been found by his parents among the scribes in the Temple, it is specifically said: 'And he went with them and came to Nazareth ... And Jesus increased in physical stature, in the noblest habits, and in wisdom.' Why are these particular attributes mentioned? It was because they could be part of his nature in a very special sense now that the Zarathustra-individuality was in him. I must call particular attention here to the fact that the words referring to the three attributes in certain translations of the Bible are sometimes as follows: 'And Jesus increased in wisdom and age and in favour with God and man.' Do we really need a Gospel to tell us that age increases in a body of twelve? Weizsäcker's translation is: 'And Jesus increased in wisdom and in stature and in favour with God and man.' But this does not convey the real meaning. The real meaning is that in the Nathan Jesus boy there was now a different individuality—one whose nature was not, as had previously been the case, purely inward, but who, having developed hitherto in a perfected physical body, was able to make himself manifest in the external physical stature as well. Furthermore, habits that are acquired from life and develop in the etheric body as their special province had previously been absent from the nature of the Nathan Jesus. His capacity for love was so great that it could be the foundation on which to build; but this capacity was a spontaneous reality and could not imprint itself into habits acquired from life. Now, however, the other individuality was present, having in his own nature the powers resulting from mature development of the physical and etheric bodies, and in these conditions it was possible for habits to come to visible expression and be impressed into the etheric body. That was the second attribute. The third, increase 'in wisdom' in the ordinary sense of the word, is easier to understand. Jesus of St Luke's Gospel was not 'wise'; he was capable of infinite, supreme love. The increase in wisdom was due to the presence in him of the Zarathustra-individuality.

In speaking about the Gospel of St Luke I referred to the fact that it is quite possible for a human being from whom the individuality has departed and who has then only the three sheaths—physical, etheric and astral—to go on living for a time. But he of whom the early chapters of St Matthew's Gospel speaks—Jesus of the Solomon line—wasted away and died, comparatively soon after his twelfth year. At first, then, there were *two* boys; then the two became *one*.

In very ancient records there are often remarkable utterances which cannot be understood unless the relevant facts are known. Later on we will go into the more intimate aspect of the union of the two boys; at the moment I will refer only to the following.

In the so-called 'Gospel of the Egyptians'[17] there is a passage which already in the early centuries of our era was regarded as extremely heretical, because Christian circles either did not want to hear the truth or did not want the truth to come to light. Something was nevertheless preserved in an apochryphal writing where it is said in effect that salvation (the Kingdom) will come to the world when the Two become One and the Outer becomes as the Inner. This sentence exactly expresses the occult reality of which I have told you. Salvation depends upon the Two becoming One. And the Two became One in very truth when in the twelfth year of his life the Zarathustra-individuality passed over into the Nathan Jesus and qualities that at first had been entirely inward became outward. The inwardness of soul in the Jesus of St Luke's Gospel was profound beyond all telling. But this quality manifested outwardly too when the Zarathustra-individuality, whose development had proceeded in the physical and etheric bodies of the Solomon Jesus, permeated that inwardness with the forces engendered by his contact with those bodies. An impulse of such power then pervaded the physical and etheric bodies of the Nathan Jesus from within that the outer could become an expression of the inner—of the inner nature as it had been before the Zarathustra-individuality had passed into the Jesus of St Luke's Gospel. The Two had become One.*

We have now followed Zarathustra from his birth as the Jesus of St Matthew's Gospel to his twelfth year, when he left his original body and passed into the bodily constitution of the Nathan Jesus; this he now developed to such a lofty stage that he was able, later on, to offer it as his own three sheaths into which the Being we call Christ might be received.

* The passage concerning the Two become One occurs in the Gospel of the Egyptians and also in the Second Epistle of Clement where it is followed by the reference to the outer becoming as the inner.

PART TWO

The Magi and their Teaching

Much has been made of in some circles regarding the visitors at the two birth scenes—'kings' and 'shepherds' as representing two different streams of human being. If we can avoid being bound by stereotypes it is still illuminating to consider the deeper reasons for this, as the next extract shows as Steiner offers a plea to the future, more spiritual development of human capabilities. This leads us on to our next major consideration—that of the Magi and who they were. We note that Matthew calls them 'wise men' and does not say there were three. This number is presumed because of the three gifts, but some Eastern Christian traditions name more—as many as twelve. Their names vary, too, which we will look at later. Although often portrayed artistically as 'kings', they were not literally kings as rulers of a kingdom but were priests of the Zoroastrian religion and bore kingly qualities as were expected and understood at that time for establishing social order. There was also a kind of Messianic prophecy in Psalm 72:11, 'May all kings fall down before him.' Zoroastrianism was a major world religion stemming from Iran, following the teacher Zarathustra (Greek: Zoroaster, meaning 'Golden Star'). It exists still in a very limited form within Iran but much larger and freer communities can be found in India today where they are known as Parsees. The sixth-century AD mosaic in the Basilica of San Vitale, Ravenna, is probably a more accurate representation of the Magi showing them wearing Persian dress. Catacomb paintings and sculptures from an even earlier period also show them thus—it would seem that the early Christians had a better understanding of their real origin.

The Magi originally came from the tribe of Medes, called Magoi by the Greeks ('Magi' is the plural of the Latin *Magus*). They were thought to have been instituted by King Cyrus in the sixth century BC when he founded a new Persian empire. They were considered 'wise men' as they studied the stars to guide their rulers, both as astronomers and astrologers, and were also often magicians—hence our word 'magic'. The Zoroastrian teaching was principally about the Sun God, the zodiac and the adversary power roughly as follows, as the sixth extract describes. It is important moreover to see this teaching in its widest context as Steiner made clear: Ahura Mazda was for the Zoroastrians the spiritual Being of the Sun—the Being of Christ before he descended into a human body.

Zarathustra, who according to Steiner lived around 6000 BC introduced what he calls the 'Ancient Persian' cultural epoch, lasting about two and a half thousand years.[18] This teacher reincarnated many times, but was a further teacher to the Babylonians and Iranians in the sixth century BC, when he was known as Zaratas or Nazaratos and was a teacher of Pythagoras. This is where outer history discovers him. Zarathustra taught of the great Sun God Ahura Mazda (later called Ohrmazd or Ormuzd), the god of light and goodness who is opposed by his evil rival Angra Mainyu or Ahriman, the god of darkness, the 'father of lies'. A fact often overlooked when the dualistic Zoroastrian religion is discussed is of an original teaching which saw a unity beyond this, which Zarathustra called 'Zervane Akerene (or Zaruana Akarana)' conceived as an infinite circle of time—sometimes represented as a serpent biting its own tail, with the powers of light woven on one side and that of darkness on the other. Eventually, though, the darkness would be conquered by Ahura Mazda (Ormuzd) travelling through this curve in space which is also a time curve stretching into past and future. Thus Zaruana Akarana or Zervane (Zurvan) became identified with the constellations of the zodiac—the movement of the sun through these was the outwardly manifesting activity of Ahura Mazda whilst the zodiac itself symbolized Zaruana Akarana. When the sun passes through the zodiac in the summer months, the daylight is longer and more radiant, bringing forces of growth to the earth, so these months were seen as belonging to Ahura Mazda, whilst the chill winter months were the province of Ahriman. Six or seven constellations belonged to Ahura Mazda and five or six to Ahriman. Their qualities were executed by lesser spiritual beings, the Amesha Spentas or Amshashpands. From this teaching Steiner derives the idea that the constellations of daylight or summer are Taurus, Gemini, Cancer, Leo, Virgo, with Aries and Libra on the borders, making seven altogether, and those of night, darkness, shadow or winter are Scorpio, Sagittarius, Capricorn, Aquarius and Pisces. Thus it arose that these five signs had in some way a connection with the forces of evil and were expected to pass through a redemption. This is a difficult theme to explain in brief: ultimately the zodiac is the outer manifestation of the hierarchy of Cherubim, lofty spiritual beings, but at a very early stage of evolution some of the Cherubim held back in a mood of renunciation, a sacrifice which ultimately allowed the possibility for evil to arise.[19] We should also stress that it is important not to fall into the 'signism' that enthusiasts of popular astrology are disposed to and declare that a person must be evilly inclined because of his or her birth sign;

horoscopes of convicted criminals show no greater preponderance of the 'dark' signs than do those of other people. In another lecture Steiner points out that these 'lower' signs are in the process of 'ascending'—but must first do so by means of the activity of human beings in order to achieve the level of the higher spiritual aspects.[20]

Can we find corroboration of the teaching about the zodiac in the surviving Zoroastrian writings? We must remember we are looking at a vast span of time in which the earlier appearance of Zarathustra would not have produced written works, but an oral teaching. Any writings would have appeared very much later; nonetheless we can find some traces of earlier beliefs. There is a Persian myth[21] that has come down to us concerning Zurvan (the zodiac) who is described as wanting a son, for which he offered a sacrifice for 1000 years, but then he doubted this power of sacrifice. From his desire and doubt he conceived twins (represented by the constellation Gemini), being undifferentiated in gender—Ohrmazd, the fulfilment of his desire and Ahriman that of his doubt. He vowed to offer his kingship to whichever was born first. Ohrmazd innocently made his brother aware of this, whereupon Ahriman ripped open Zurvan's womb and declared himself as Ohrmazd. Zurvan said, 'My son is light and fragrant but you are dark and stinking.' Ahriman begins his life with a lie, but Zurvan is not deceived. When Ohrmazd appeared he offered him the symbol of the priesthood, the 'barsom' twigs which later became sacred to the magi, and in order not to break his vow, he gave Ahriman the rule of the earth for 9000 years, and to Ohrmazd the power to create the heavens and the earth. Ahriman created his demons, and when Ohrmazd had created the heavens Ahriman intervened: 'Afterwards, the evil spirit, with the confederate demons, went towards the luminaries, and he saw the sky; and he led them up, fraught with malicious intentions. He stood upon one third of the inside of the sky, and he sprang, like a snake, out of the sky down to the earth.'[22] 'Thereupon came Angra Mainya (Ahriman), who is all death, and he counter-created by his witchcraft the serpent in the river and and winter.'[23]

Given this knowledge of the cosmic struggle between good and evil, it becomes clearer as to why the three Wise Men had to encounter evil in the person of King Herod. It might be asked that if they were so wise and had special capacities why they did not perceive Herod's duplicity. They may have expected a king in Judea to be honourable but even if they did perceive his wicked nature they may have felt that he should be given the chance to resist temptation and make good. It would have been a misuse of their magical powers to try to compel him with sorcery. This part of the story raises the difficult question of the 'role' of evil in evolution. Thus here we are far from the peaceful 'paradisaical' birth story of Luke and must recognize a darker world. However, 6 January, traditionally the day of the Magi's visit, was also 30 years later the date for the Baptism, during which the redemptive power of the Christ entered into the sheaths of Jesus of Nazareth.

M.J.

5. *Basel, 23 December 1920*

The coming of Christ, of Jesus, is proclaimed to two types of human being at the Christmas festival, though of course these two embody the same, single humanity: the poor, untutored shepherds in the field, who possess only simple common sense and a simple sensibility; and the wise kings from the Orient, that is, from the land of wisdom. To these latter the coming of Christ is proclaimed through their highest grasp of wisdom, their reading in the script of the stars. Thus Christ Jesus' coming is proclaimed both to simple shepherd souls and in the loftiest wisdom of the three Magi from the Orient. The profoundest meaning lies in this contrast of a proclamation to simple shepherds on the one hand and to the wisest of the wise on the other.

Let us look at each of these kinds of annunciation. The shepherds have an inner vision of the bright angel. Their faculty of inner sight is awoken, their clairaudience is awoken. They hear the profound words which will become for them the meaning of earthly life in future times; the God in the heights is revealed to them, and they learn of the peace that will hold sway among human beings of good will on earth. Without possessing any learning or wisdom, these poor, simple shepherds, through a capacity that rises up in their souls, have a feeling experience of what is revealed to the world. And the three Magi from the Orient have the same revelation, but in their case by perfecting the wisdom that could be achieved until the time of the Mystery of Golgotha—by the subtlest observation of the passage and courses of the stars. The shepherds read within the human heart, penetrating to its profoundest depths where they become clairvoyant, so that the power of their heart's vision reveals to them the advent of humanity's Saviour. The kings, on the other hand, gaze upwards to the whole broad canopy of the heavens. They know the secrets of breadths of space and evolution through time, and have achieved a wisdom enabling them to sense and decipher these secrets of space and time; and here the Christmas mystery is revealed to them.

This tells us that what lives within us and what lives outside us in breadths of space flows from the same source. Both forms of vision were declining in the period leading up to the Mystery of Golgotha. The clairvoyant powers rising from human hearts were still strong enough in the shepherds, as the story tells, for them to hear the angels' voices singing of God revealed in the heights, in the heavens, and of peace on earth among people of good will. The shepherds, whom karma or destiny had led to the place where Christ was born, still possessed the last vestiges, if you like, of a clairvoyance arising from inner piety. And then this Christmas mystery was revealed, too, in the last vestiges of primordial sacred wisdom which in post-Atlantean times first flourished in the ancient Indian civilization, then especially amongst the Persians, and subsequently the Chaldeans, and which still lived on in a culture to which the three Magi of the Orient belonged—a very ancient, primordial wisdom which encompassed the world in its dimension of time and space, a wisdom to whose loftiest realms these wise Magi could still raise themselves. But in the fifth post-Atlantean epoch both these sources of wisdom were failing.

What led to inner vision in the poor shepherds and to insight into the mysteries of space and time in the wise kings of the Orient is now no longer alive in humanity in general. We have been obliged instead to discover the human being as such, unaided and dependent on his own resources. As humanity we have been obliged to pass through times bereft of the divine, so as to find freedom in the lonely, abandoned condition of human existence. But we must find our way back again to a connection, on the one hand, with the highest wisdom of the Magi from the Orient, and on the other with the deeper vision emerging from the shepherds' hearts in the angels' annunciation.

All powers evolve. What has become today of the clairvoyant intelligence which the wise kings of the Orient developed into their astrology, their own form of astronomy? We fail to understand human evolution if we do not study such things. Today this knowledge has become our abstract arts of mathematics and geometry. The abstract forms nowadays taught in school in geometry and mathematics are the last realms of capacities whose living glories and cosmic light were mastered by the ancient wisdom that led the three Magi to Christ. Outer vision has become an inner faculty of thinking about spatial and temporal relationships. Whereas the Magi of the East were capable of calculating when the Saviour would be born, using their seership to decipher the mysteries of space, our modern astronomers, their successors, merely calculate future eclipses of the sun or moon and suchlike. And whereas the poor shepherds in the field raised themselves in inwardness of heart to a vision of something far removed from them, a vision of the Christmas mystery, the capacity to hear the heavenly annunciation, all that remains to modern humankind today is perception of external, sensory nature. The simplicity of the shepherds has developed into and been succeeded by external sensory perception, in the same way that astronomers' calculation of future eclipses has succeeded the wisdom of the three Magi.

The shepherds in the fields were equipped with deepened feeling, a heart vision that allowed them to perceive the Christmas mystery. Our contemporaries today are equipped with telescope and microscope. But no telescope or microscope will give us insight, as the shepherds' hearts did, into what solves humankind's deepest riddle. No prediction made possible by calculations of sun and moon eclipses will enable us to grasp the course of world evolution as did the star wisdom of the Magi from the Orient. It is wonderful to experience how all that has been sundered and differentiated within humanity flows together again in unified human feeling when we see that the untutored experience of the shepherds, in the piety of their hearts, is the same as what came to expression in the highest wisdom of the Magi from the Orient. And it is marvellous to see how these two realities are placed side by side in Christian tradition.

The two paths which enabled humanity to understand the birth of Christ have been lost in modern times. We have returned from the crib to the Christmas tree, to the tree of paradise, and from the Christ who belongs to all humanity to national gods, who are merely so many Yahwehs and not Christ.

But just as the profoundest depths of our being reveal what is a common possession of all humankind, so equally true is the fact that this common possession is revealed through all breadths of space and all mysteries of time. In the depths of our being is something which speaks only of our humanness and erases all human differences. Only there, in these depths, do we find the Christ. And a wisdom exists that encompasses the world as a unity, encompasses space and time, and is greater than all other wisdom relating to distinct and separate aspects of existence. And this is the star wisdom that leads us to Christ. What enabled the shepherds on the one hand and the Magi on the other to find their way to Christ Jesus is today needed again in a new form. In other words, we need to deepen our external perception of nature through what the human heart can develop as spiritual insight into the natural world. Powers that arise from the piety and reverence of the human heart must lead us to perceive what at present we only scrutinize through microscopes, telescopes, X-rays and so forth. If we do so then growing plants, the rushing river, the bubbling spring, the lightning and thunder in the skies will no longer be something we observe with indifference but instead all will speak to us. Meadow flowers, the lightning and thunder in the clouds, shining stars and radiant sun will stream into our eyes, ears and hearts in words that are a kind of summation of all our perception of nature, announcing to us nothing less than the revelation of God in the heavenly heights, of the peace that will come to human beings of good will on earth.

A time must come when observation of the natural world emerges from the arid, prosaic, clinical mode as practised in laboratories, and is revitalized by a quality we can no longer acquire as the shepherds in Bethlehem did, but that will be vouchsafed to us in the utterances of plants, animals, stars, springs and rivers. The whole of nature, you see, proclaims what the angel of annunciation uttered: that God is revealed in the heavenly heights, and peace can come among human beings of good will on earth.

We need what the Magi acquired from their observation of the stars, and must awaken it within us. Just as we must hearken to nature outside us, learning to hear the angels sing again from the surrounding natural world, so likewise we must become able to gain from within us an astronomy, a solving of the riddle of the cosmos, through Imagination, Inspiration and Intuition. We need to develop a science of the spirit, an esoteric science that draws upon our inner human nature. We must fathom the nature of our own intrinsic being, and this being must speak to us from world evolution through the mysteries of Saturn, Sun, Moon, Earth, Jupiter, Venus and Vulcan.[24] We must feel a universe arising within us. Since the Mystery of Golgotha, our vision of the profoundest mysteries of the world has undergone a reversal, an inversion.

6. *Berlin, 19 January 1911*

When we turn our attention to Zarathustra we find that we must look back over an extremely long period. According to certain modern researches, he is considered to be a contemporary of the Buddha, the approximate date of his life being fixed at some six to six and a half centuries before the birth of Christianity. It is, however, a remarkable and interesting fact that other investigators of late years, after carefully studying all existing traditions concerning Zarathustra, have been driven to the conclusion that the personality concealed beneath the name of the ancient founder of Persian religion must have lived a great many centuries before the time of the Buddha. Greek historians have stated over and over again that the period ascribed to Zarathustra should be put back very many, possibly five to six thousand, years before the Trojan War [the date of which has been placed at about 1200 BC] . . .

These things Zarathustra impressed earnestly and clearly upon his disciples, and, using simple words, we can picture him as addressing them somewhat as follows: 'When you regard man, you must realize that he does not only consist of a material body—such is but an outer expression of the spirit which is within. Even as the physical covering is a manifestation in condensed and crystallized form of the true spiritual man, so is the sun, which appears to us as a light-giving mass when considered as such, merely the external manifestation of an inner spiritual sun.' In the same way as we term the human spirit element as distinguished from the physical the 'aura', to use an ancient expression, so do we call the all-embracing hidden spiritual part of the sun the Great Aura (Aura Mazda), in contradistinction to man's spiritual component, which is sometimes called the 'Little aura'.

Now, Zarathustra named all that lies hidden within and beyond man's mere apprehension of the physical sun—'Aura Mazda' or 'Ahura Mazda'—and considered this element as important to our spiritual experiences and conditions, as is the physical sun to the well-being of plants and animals, and all that lives upon the face of the earth. There behind the physical sun lies the Spiritual Master—the Creator—'Ahura Mazda' or 'Aura Mazda', and from 'Ahura Mazda' came the name, 'Ormuzd' or the 'Spirit of Light'.

While the Indians mystically searched their inner being in order to attain to Brahma—the Eternal—who shines outward as a point of light from within man's essence, Zarathustra urged his disciples to turn their eyes upon the great periphery of existence, and pointed out that there within the body of the sun dwells the great Solar Spirit—Ahura Mazda—the 'Spirit of Light'. He taught them that, just in the same way as when man strives to raise his spirit to perfection, so must he ever battle against his lower passions and desires, against the delusive images suggested by possible deception and falsehood, and all those antagonistic influences within, which continually oppose his spiritual impulses. Thus must 'Ahura Mazda' face the opposition of the 'Spirit of Darkness'—'Angra Mainyu[25]' or 'Ahriman'.

We can now realize how the great Zarathustrian conception could be evolved from experiences born of sensations and sense contents. Through these, Zarathustra could advance his disciples to a point where he could make clear to them that within man there is a 'Perfecting Principle', which tells him that whatever may be his present condition this principle will work persistently within, and through it he may raise himself ever higher and higher; but at the same time there also operate impulses and inclinations, deceit and falsehood, all tending towards imperfection. This Perfecting Principle must therefore be developed and expanded, in order that the world may be destined to attain to wiser and more advanced states of perfection; it is the 'Principle of Ahura Mazda', and is assailed throughout the whole world of Ahriman—the 'Spirit of Darkness'—who through imperfection and evil brings shadows into the light. By following the method above outlined, Zarathustra's disciples were enabled to realize and to feel that in truth each individual man is an image of the outer universe.

We must not seek the true significance of such teaching in theories, concepts and ideas, but in active vivid consciousness and in the sensations impressed when through it man realizes that he is so related to the universe that he can say: 'As I stand here, I am a small world, and as such I am a replica of the great cosmos.' Just as we have within us a principle of perfection, and another which is antagonistic, so throughout the universe is Ormuzd opposed by Ahriman. In these teachings the whole cosmos is represented as typical of a widespread human being; the forces of greatest virtue are termed Ahura Mazda, while against these operate the powers of Angra Mainyu.

When a person realizes that he is in direct contact with the workings of the universe and the attendant physical phenomena but can only apprehend the perceptual, then as he begins to gain spiritual experience a feeling of awe may come over him (especially if he is materialistic in thought) when he learns through spectrum analysis that the same matter which exists upon the earth is found in the most distant stars. It is the same with Zarathustrianism, when man feels that his spiritual part is merged in that of the whole cosmos, and that he has indeed emanated from its great spirit. Herein lies the true significance of such a doctrine, which was not merely abstract in character but on the contrary wholly concrete.

In this present age it is most difficult to make people understand (even when they have a certain sense for the spiritual that lies behind the perceptual) that it is necessary to a true and spiritually scientific view of the cosmos that there be more than one central unity of spirit-power. But even as we distinguish between the separate forces in nature, such as heat, light and chemical forces, so in the world of spirit must we recognize not merely one centralized power (whose existence is not denied) but we must differentiate between it and certain subservient uplifting forces, whose spheres of action are more circumscribed than are those of the all-embracing spirit. Thus it was that Zarathustra made a distinction between the omnipotent Ormuzd, and those spirit beings by whom he was served.

Before we turn to a consideration of these subservient spirit entities, we must draw attention to the fact that the Zarathustrian theory was not a mere dualism, a simple doctrine of two worlds—the worlds of Ormuzd and of Ahriman—but that it maintained that underlying this double flux of cosmic influence is a definite unity, a single power, which gave birth to both the Realm of Light (Ormuzd) and to the Realm of Darkness (Ahriman). It is not easy to gain a right understanding of Zarathustra's conception concerning this 'unity' underlying Ormuzd and Ahriman. With reference to this point the Greek authors state that the ancient Persians worshipped and regarded as a 'living unity' that which lay beyond the light, and which Zarathustra termed 'Zervane Akerene'. How can we gain a comprehension of what Zarathustra in his teachings meant by 'Zervane Akerene' or 'Zaruana Akarana'?

Let us consider for a moment the course of evolution; this we must regard as of such a nature that all beings tend towards greater and greater perfection. So that if we look into the future we see more and more of the radiance from the Light Realms of Ormuzd; but if we turn our eyes upon the past we realize how the powers of Ahriman, which oppose Ormuzd, are circumstanced, and we then know that with the passing of time these must be conquered and for ever ended.

We will now picture to ourselves that the path into the future and that into the past each lead to the same point—a conception which present-day man finds most difficult to grasp. Let us take as an example a circle. If we pass along the circumference from the lowest point in one direction, we come to the opposite point above; if, however, we go along the other side, we come to the same point. When we consider a larger circle, then the circumference is flatter, and we must traverse a greater distance in each case. We will now suppose a circle to expand ever more and more; then ultimately the path on either side becomes a straight line, and is infinite. But just before the circle becomes infinite we would reach the same point whether we went by the one path or the other. Why, then, should not the same happen when the circumference is so flattened that the periphery becomes a straight line? In this case the point at infinity on the one must be identical with that on the other, and therefore we must be able to travel to it, from the lowest point in one sense (say, positive), and return as if coming from the opposite (negative) direction. This means that when our conception is infinite we have a straight line extending without limit on either side, but which is in reality the circumference of an infinite circle.

The abstraction given above lies at the basis of Zarathustra's conception of what he termed Zaruana Akarana. Here, with regard to time, we look in one direction into the future, in the other into the past, and when we consider an infinite period, time closes in upon itself as in a circle. This self-contained and infinite time circle is symbolically represented as a serpent eternally biting its own tail, and into it is woven upon the one side the Power of Light, shedding upon us continually a greater and greater radiance; and upon the other, the Power of Darkness, becoming ever more and more profound. When we are midway, then is the light (Ormuzd) intermingled with the shadows (Ahriman); all is interwoven in the self-embracing, infinite flux of time, 'Zaruana Akarana'.

There is something more about this ancient cosmic conception; its basic ideas were treated seriously, there were no mere vague statements such as: 'Without and remote from all that is material in this perceptual world—beyond those things which affect our eyes, our ears, and sense organs in general—abides the Spirit.' But it was definitely asserted that in everything which could be seen and apprehended therein could be discerned something of the nature of spirit signs, or a manifestation of the spirit-world.

If we take a sheet of paper upon which are inscribed alphabetical characters, these may be combined into words; but we must first have learnt how to read. Without this ability no one could read about Zarathustra, for they would merely perceive certain characters which could only be followed with the eyes. Actual reading can only take place after it is clearly understood how to connect such characters with that which is within the soul. Now, Zarathustra discerned a written sign underlying all that was in the perceptual world, particularly in the manner in which the stars are grouped in the universe. Just as we recognize written characters upon paper, so did Zarathustra descry in the starry firmament something similar to letters, conveying a message from the spirit-world. Hence arose an art of penetrating into the world of spirit, and of deciphering the signs indicated by the arrangement of the stars, and of finding a method of reading and construing from their movements and order in what manner and way those spiritual beings that are without, inscribe the facts concerning their activities in space.

Zarathustra and his disciples had a paramount interest in these matters. To them it was a most important sign that Ahura Mazda, in order to accomplish his creations and to reveal his message to the world, should (in the language of modern astronomy) 'describe a circular path'. This fact was regarded as a sign traced in the heavens indicating in what manner Ahura Mazda worked, and the relation which his activities bore to the universe as a whole. It is important that Zarathustra was able to point out that the constellations of the zodiac, taken together as forming a closed curve in space, should symbolize a continuous and also retroactive time flux; and we can realize that there is indeed a most profound significance underlying the statement that one branch of this time-curve stretches outward into the future while the other leads backward into the remote past. Zaruana Akarana is that bright band of stars, later known as the zodiac, that self-contained timeline ever traversed by Ormuzd, the Spirit of Light. In other words, the passage of the sun across the constellations of the zodiac is an expression of the activity of

Ormuzd, while the zodiac itself is the symbol of Zaruana Akarana. In reality, Zaruana Akarana and the zodiac are identical terms, just in the same way as are Ormuzd and Ahura Mazda.

There are two special circumstances to be considered in this connection. First is when the passage of the sun through the zodiac takes place while it is light, as in the summer. At such time the solar radiance falls full upon the earth, bringing with it the power emanating from those spiritual forces ever flowing outward, from the light-realms of Ormuzd. That part of the zodiac traversed by Ahura Mazda in the daytime, or during the summer, denotes the manner in which He works and weaves unhindered by Ahriman. On the other hand, those zodiacal constellations which lie far beneath the horizon—dark regions through which we might picture the passage of Angra Mainyu—are symbolical of the kingdom of the shadows.

We have stated that Zarathustra regarded Ormuzd as associated with the bright sections of the zodiac (Zaruana Akarana), while he looked upon Ahriman as connected with the gloom. In what way do the activities of Ormuzd and Ahriman find expression in our material world? In order to understand this point we must realize that the effect of the solar rays is different in the morning from that at noon, varying as the sun ascends from Aries to Taurus, and again during its descent towards the horizon. The influence exerted is not the same in winter as in summer, and differs with every passing sign of the zodiac. Zarathustra regarded the changing aspects of the sun in connection with the zodiacal constellations as symbolical of the activities of Ormuzd proceeding from different directions, and from which came those spiritual beings that are both His servants and His sons, and who are ready at all times to execute His commands. These are the 'Amshaspands' or 'Amesha Spentas', subservient entities, to each of whom is allotted some special duty.

While Ormuzd controls all active functions in the light-realms, the Amshaspands undertake that specific work which finds expression in the transmission of the sun's light when in Aries, Taurus, Cancer, etc. But the true vital activity of Ormuzd is manifested in the full radiance of the sun, shining throughout all bright signs of the zodiac, from Aries to Libra or Scorpio. Following the Zarathustrian line of thought, we might say: 'It is as though the evil powers of Ahriman came through the earth from those dark regions where abide his servants—his own Amshaspands—who are opposed to the good genii standing by the side of Ormuzd.' Zarathustra actually distinguished between twelve different subservient spirit entities: six or seven on the side of Ormuzd, and five or six on that of Ahriman. These are regarded as typical of good or evil genii (Amesha Spentas—lower spirits), according as to whether their influence comes with the sun's rays from the bright signs of the zodiac or emanates from those which are in gloom.

The Star of the Magi and their Gifts

Much speculation has been given to the nature of the guiding 'star'. One theory is that the Magi perceived the triple conjunction of the planets Jupiter and Saturn in 7 BC, a view made famous by Kepler. Then Jupiter moved from the previous 'royal' constellation of Leo into Virgo between 3 BC and early January 1 BC, which is where Ormond Edwards dates the arrival of the Wise Men. This planetary event no doubt alerted them to the possibility of a significant event, especially as Leo was Judaea's special constellation, but it is not *the* star—neither was it a comet. Steiner makes it clear in a previous extract that this was not an astronomical star but was a clairvoyant experience of the descending soul of their former teacher who had prophesied his return. In the second extract that follows, it would seem that the Christ power also shone through it. Prophecies of Zarathustra's return were noted by some early Christian writers. This one was included by the Syriac writer Theodore bar Konai in the eighth century AD and is abridged from Andrew Welburn's remarkable study of Zarathustra's incarnations, *The Book with Fourteen Seals.*[26]

> Zarathustra was sitting by the spring of water called Glosha of Hourin... And he opened his mouth and spoke in the presence of his disciples Vishtaspa, Saena and Medyomah: 'I tell you, O my friends and my children ... hear, and I will reveal to you a great mystery concerning the Great King who is to come into the world... He will open the way into the depths of the

> earth, and from the depths he will ascend into the heights ... for he is the Child begotten of the Word which created all things.' ... Vishtaspa said to Zarathustra: 'The one of whom you have spoken—whence comes his power? Is he One Greater than you, or are you the Greater One than he?'
>
> Zarathustra said to him: 'He will arise from my family and line. He is I, and I am He. I am in him, and he is in me. When the beginning of his coming appears, great signs will appear in heaven. There will be a brilliant star in the midst of the firmament, whose light will surpass that of the sun... And when the star of which I have spoken rises, let ambassadors be sent by you, bearing gifts, to worship him and give him your gifts ... I and he are one.'

It could be said that Christian writers compiled these statements 'after the event' but Andrew Welburn comments that this text has many Zoroastrian touches and his scholarly work gives a much broader and deeper picture as he examines in it the first century BC text The Apocalypse of Adam.

The three Magi have often been portrayed as coming from different races and countries. This is not necessarily a contradiction and is important for showing the inclusive nature of the birth of Jesus and for the future of human evolution. In the first extract Rudolf Steiner describes them as being representatives of much older, so-called 'root' races of humanity. These comments are referring to very ancient times and should not at all be taken to refer to present-day races. The third extract stresses the unifying power of Christ for humanity in the future, represented by the visit of the Magi.

Their gifts—uncommon ones for a newborn baby—also carry significant meanings as the extracts show. Generally they are summed up as 'gold for a king, frankincense for a priest, myrrh for a healer', but sometimes also as representing thinking (gold), feeling (frankincense) and will (myrrh). Gold was originally densified from the etheric sun substance and is traditionally connected with thinking and wisdom, and is a metal sacred to royalty. Frankincense is a gum resin from trees found in Arabia and Somaliland. It was a ceremonial incense and holy oil for the Jews and Babylonians, and is still used by Parsees and of course in Christian churches where incense is burnt. Myrrh is also a gum resin from bushes in the same regions and around the Red Sea. In fact recent conflicts in these areas have made the harvesting of these resins more difficult, affecting local people's livelihoods. It is acrid and bitter but also used in Jewish holy oil and in the *Kyphi* of the Egyptians for embalming. It has cleansing, antiseptic properties and has long been associated with death, sacrifice and resurrection. The words of the carol *We Three Kings* by John Henry Hopkins Jr. in 1857 well sum up these qualities.

M.J.

7. *Bern, 6 September 1910*

Zarathustra himself incarnated later on in other astral and etheric bodies. Of particular interest to us is his incarnation as Zarathas or Nazarathos in ancient Chaldea in the sixth century BC, where the Chaldean sages were his pupils and where the wisest among the pupils of the occult schools of the Hebrews at the time of the Babylonian captivity came into contact with him. The pupils of the Chaldean occult schools were then occupied throughout the following six centuries with the traditions, rites and cults originating with Zarathustra in the personality of Zarathas or Nazarathos. All the generations of pupils—Chaldean, Babylonian, Assyrian and so on—who were living in those regions of Asia deeply revered the name of this great master. They waited with longing for his next incarnation, for they knew that after six hundred years he would come again. The secret of his coming was known to them and was like a beacon light shining in from the future.

And as the time approached when the blood would be suitably prepared for the new incarnation of Zarathustra, the three envoys, the three wise Magi, set out from the East; they knew that the revered name of Zarathustra himself would lead them as a star to the place where his new incarnation was to take place. It was the being of the great teacher himself who as the 'star' led the three Magi to the birthplace of the Jesus of St Matthew's Gospel. Ordinary philology itself will confirm that the word 'star' was used in ancient times to denote human individuality. It is not only spiritual research which from its own sources tells us more clearly than anything else that the three Magi at that time were led by Zoroaster, the 'golden star', to the place where he was to reincarnate, but it follows from the very use of the word 'star' for human individualities of lofty development that the star by which the Wise Men were guided was Zarathustra himself.

Thus six hundred years before the Christian era the Magi of the East had come into contact with the individuality who subsequently incarnated as the Jesus of St Matthew's Gospel. Now Zarathustra himself led them to Palestine and they followed in his track. For it was the star of Zarathustra moving towards Palestine that guided the Magi along their way from the Chaldean mysteries in the East, to Palestine, where Zarathustra was about to incarnate.

This secret of the coming incarnation of Zarathustra, of Zarathas or Nazarathos, was known in the mysteries of Chaldea. But the secret of the blood of the Hebrew people, which was that when the time was ripe it would be suitable for the new bodily constitution of Zarathustra—this was a teaching of the Essenes, who in their mysteries were transported in soul through the 42 Stages.

Thus there were, to begin with, two groups who knew something about the secret of the Jesus of St Matthew's Gospel: the Chaldean initiates, who possessed knowledge relating to the individuality of Zarathustra and his coming incarnation in Hebrew blood, and the sect of the Essenes, which was concerned with another aspect of the physical constitution, of the blood of the coming Being.

8. *Berlin, 30 December 1904*

You will remember that I have spoken of the meaning of the Christmas festival in its connection with the evolution of races, that is, the epochs of civilization, and of how its significance lies in this very connection, both with respect to the past and the future.

I want to speak today about a festival which in modern times is considered less important than the Christmas festival itself: the festival of the Three Kings, of the Magi who came from the East to greet the newly born Jesus. This festival of the Epiphany (celebrated on the 6th of January) will assume greater and greater significance as its true symbolism comes to be understood.

It will be obvious to you that very profound symbolism is contained in the festival of the three Magi from the East. Until the fifteenth century this symbolism was kept very secret and no clear indications about it were given. But since that century some light has been thrown on the festival of the Magi by exoteric descriptions. One of the Three Kings, *Caspar*, is portrayed as a Moor, an inhabitant of Africa; one as a white man, a European, *Melchior*; and one, *Balthazar*, as an Asiatic, for the colour of his skin is that of an inhabitant of India. They bring myrrh, gold and frankincense as offerings to the child Jesus in Bethlehem.

These three offerings are full of meaning and in keeping with the whole symbolism of the festival celebrated on the 6th of January. The date itself throws some light on a festival which is very important esoterically. The 6th of January is the same date as that on which, in ancient Egypt, the festival of

Osiris was celebrated, the festival of the re-finding of Osiris. As you know, Osiris was overcome by his enemy Typhon: Isis seeks and eventually finds him. This re-finding of Osiris, the son of God, is represented in the festival of the 6th of January. The festival of the three kings is the same festival, but in its Christian form. It was also celebrated among the Assyrians, the Armenians and the Phoenicians. Everywhere it was connected with a kind of universal baptism—with a rebirth out of water. This in itself points to the connection with the re-finding of Osiris.

What does the disappearance of Osiris signify? It signifies the transition from the times *before* the middle of the Lemurian epoch[27] to the times *after* the middle of that epoch. Before the middle of the Lemurian epoch, no human being was endowed with Manas (Spirit Self). It was not until the middle of the epoch that Manas came down into human beings as a fertile seed. Manas was given to humanity; and in each single individual a grave was created for it—for the dismembered Osiris. The divine Manas was disseminated and thereafter dwelt in human beings. In the Egyptian mystery-language, human bodies were called the 'graves of Osiris'—Manas was fettered until it was freed by the new revelation of *love*.

What is the new revelation, the new manifestation of love? The descent of Manas somewhere around the middle of the Lemurian epoch was accompanied by the penetration into mankind of the element of desire, or passion. Before that time there had been no desire as such. The animals of the preceding epochs were cold-blooded; even man himself at that time had no warm blood. The human beings of the Old Moon period and, correspondingly, of the Third Earth Round, may be likened to fishes in the sense that they possessed the same degree of warmth as their environment. Of this epoch the Bible says: 'The Spirit of God brooded over the waters.' The principle of love was then not *within* beings, but outside, manifesting as earthly Kama (that is to say, earthly passion or desire). Kama is egoistic love. The first bringer of love free of all egoism is Christ who appeared in the body of Jesus of Nazareth.

Who are the Magi? They represent the initiates of the three preceding races or epochs of culture, the initiates of mankind up to the time of the coming of Christ, who is the bringer of love free of egoism—the resurrected Osiris. The initiates, and the three Magi also, were endowed with Manas. They bring gold, frankincense and myrrh as their offerings. And why are their skins of three colours: white, yellow and black? One is European, his skin is white; one is Indian, his skin is yellow; one is African, his skin is black. This shows their connection with the so-called root races. The remaining survivors of the Lemurian race are black; those of the Atlantean race are yellow; and the representatives of the Fifth Root Race, the post-Atlantean or Aryan race, are white.

Thus the Three Kings or Magi are representatives of the Lemurians, the Atlanteans and the Aryans. They bring three offerings. The European (Melchior) brings gold, the symbol of wisdom, of intelligence, which comes to expression above all in the Fifth Root Race. The offering of the initiate representing the Fourth Root Race (Balthazar) is frankincense, connected with what was intrinsically characteristic of the Atlanteans. They were united more directly with the Godhead, a union which took effect as a suggestive influence, a kind of universal hypnosis. This union with the Godhead is symbolized by the offering: feeling must be sublimated in order that God may make it fruitful. Frankincense is the universal symbol for what has to do with Intuition.

In the language of esotericism, myrrh is the symbol of dying, of death. What is the meaning of dying and of resurrection, as exemplified in the resurrected Osiris? I refer you here to words of Goethe:

> As long as you have not grasped
> Life issuing forth from death,
> You're but a troubled guest
> Upon the shrouded earth.

Jacob Boehme expresses the same thought in the words: 'He who dies not before he dies perishes when he dies.' Myrrh is the symbol of the dying of the lower life and the resurrection of the higher life. It is offered by the initiate representing the Third Root Race (Lemurian). A deep meaning lies in this. Jesus of Nazareth is a very highly developed individuality. In the thirtieth year of his life he gives up his own life to the descending Christ, the descending Logos. All this the Magi foresaw. The great sacrifice made by Jesus of Nazareth is that he gave up his I to make way for the Second Logos[28] ...

... Myrrh is the symbol of sacrifice, of death, the sacrifice of the earthly in order that a higher principle may come to life. In the middle of the Lemurian epoch, Osiris came to his grave; Manas entered human beings who were then educated under the guidance of the initiates until the principle of love (Buddhi) could shine forth in Christ Jesus. Buddhi is the heavenly love. The lower, sexual principle is ennobled through the love brought by Christ. Kama is purified in the fire of divine love.

Melchior is the representative of the principle of wisdom,

of intelligence—the task of the Fifth Root Race. This is symbolized by his offering, gold.

Frankincense symbolizes the principle of sacramental offering, dominant in the Fourth Root Race, the Atlantean. The task of Christianity will find fulfilment in the Sixth Root Race, when material existence will once more be permeated with ritual and sacrament. Sacraments have very largely lost their meaning today; the feeling for their significance has disappeared. But this feeling will be rekindled when the higher being of man is born. It is this that is symbolized by the frankincense.

In the Lemurian Root Race, Osiris meets his death, in the Sixth Root Race, Osiris is resurrected.

Thus the offerings made by the Three Kings indicate the connection of the festival with the Third, Fourth, Fifth and Sixth Root Races. By what are the Three Holy Kings guided, and whither are they led? They are guided by a star to a grotto, a cave in Bethlehem. This is something that can be understood only by one who has knowledge of the so-called lower, or astral, mysteries. To be led by a star means nothing else than to see the soul itself as a star. But when is the soul seen as a star? When one can behold the soul as a radiant aura. But what kind of aura is so radiant that it can be a guide? There is the aura that glimmers with only a feeble light; such an aura cannot guide. There is a higher aura, that of the intelligence, which has, it is true, a flowing, up-surging light, but is not yet able to guide. But the bright aura, aglow with Buddhi, is in very truth a star, is a radiant guide. In Christ, the star of Buddhi lights up—the star which accompanies the evolution of mankind. The light that shines before the Magi is the soul of Christ Himself. The Second Logos Himself shines before the Magi and over the cave in Bethlehem.

The grotto or cave is the body in which the soul dwells. The seer beholds the body from within. In astral vision everything is reversed—for example, 365 instead of 563. The human body is seen as a cave. In the body of Jesus shines the Christ star, the soul of Christ. This must be conceived as a reality, taking place in the astral world. It is an enactment of the lesser mysteries. There, in very truth, the Christ Soul shines as an auric star, and it is by this star that the initiates of the three Root Races are led to Jesus in Bethlehem.

The festival of the Three Kings is celebrated every year on the 6th of January, and its significance will steadily increase. People will come to understand more and more what a magus is, and what the great magi, the masters, are. And then understanding of Christianity will lead to understanding of spiritual science.

9. Cologne, 25 December 1907

If you were in the Cathedral last night you could have seen written there in illuminated lettering: C, M, B. As you will all know, these letters represent the names of the so-called Three Holy Kings, according to the tradition of the Christian Church: Caspar, Melchior, Balthazar. These names awaken quite special memories for Cologne. An old legend tells us that some time after they had become bishops and died their bones had been brought here. Another legend relates that a Danish king had once come to Cologne, bringing with him three crowns for the Three Holy Kings. After he had returned home he had a dream; in his dream the Three Kings appeared to him and offered him three chalices: the first chalice contained gold, the second frankincense, and the third one myrrh. When the Danish king awoke the Three Kings had vanished, but the chalices remained; they stood before him—the three gifts which he had retained from his dream.

In this legend there is profound meaning. We are to understand that the king in his dream attained a certain insight into the spiritual world by which he learnt the symbolic meaning of these Three Kings, these Three Wise Men of the East who brought offerings of gold, frankincense and myrrh at the birth of Christ Jesus. And from this realization he retained a lasting possession: those three human virtues which are symbolized in the gold, the frankincense and the myrrh: self-knowledge in the gold; self-piety, that is the piety of the innermost self—which we can self-surrender—in the frankincense; and in the myrrh self-consummation and self-development, or the preservation of the eternal in the self.

It was possible for the king to receive these three virtues as gifts from another world because he had endeavoured to penetrate with his whole soul into the profound symbol lying concealed in the Three Kings who brought their offerings to Christ Jesus.

There are many features in this legend which lead us a long way towards understanding the Christ-principle, and what it is to bring about in the world. Among its profound features are the Adoration and the Presentation by the three Magi, the three oriental Kings, and only with the deepest understanding may we approach this fundamental symbolism of the Christian tradition. Later the idea was formed that the first King was the representative of the Asiatic races; the second, the representative of the European peoples; and the third, the representative of the African races. Wherever people wanted to understand Christianity as the religion of earthly harmony they saw in the Three Kings and their homage a union of the different lines of thought and religious movements in the world into the one principle, the Christian principle. When this legend received this form those who had penetrated into the principles of esoteric Christianity saw in Christianity not only a force which had affected the course of human development, but they saw in the being embodied in Jesus of Nazareth a cosmic world-force—a force far transcending the merely human that prevails in this present age. They saw in the Christ-principle a force that indeed represents for mankind a human ideal lying in a far distant future, an ideal which can only be approached by our understanding the whole world more and more in the spirit. They saw in man, in the first place, a miniature being, a miniature world, a microcosm, an image of the macrocosm, the great, all-embracing world. This macrocosm comprises all that man can perceive with his external senses, see with his eyes, hear with his ears, but comprises, besides, all that the spirit could perceive from the perceptions of the least developed human spirit up to perceptions in the spiritual world. This was how the esoteric Christian of the earliest times regarded the world . . .

We see that all forms of life which desire to unfold their external physical power look up to the sun when the sun rises in the sky in spring and strive to receive the external physical power of the sun. But when on a summer noon the sun's physical power pours most lavishly onto the earth its spiritual power is weakest. In the winter midnight, however, when the sun rays the least physical power down to the earth, man can see the sun's spirit through the earth, which has become transparent for him. The esoteric Christian felt that through absorption in Christian esotericism he approached more and more that power of inward vision through which he could imbue his feeling, thinking and his will-impulses in gazing into this spiritual sun. Then the mystery-novice was led to a vision of the greatest importance. As long as the earth is opaque the separate parts appear inhabited by people of different confessions, but the unifying bond is not there. Human races are as scattered as the climates. Human opinions are scattered all over the earth and there is no connecting link. But to the degree in which people begin to look through the earth into the sun by their inner power of vision, to the degree in which the 'star' appears to them through the earth, their confessions will flow together to one great united Brotherhood. And those who guided the great separated human masses in the truth of the higher planes, towards their initiation into the higher worlds, were known as 'Magi'. They were three in number, as in the various parts of the earth various powers express themselves. Humanity had, therefore, to be led in different ways. But as a unifying power there appears the star, rising beyond the earth. It leads the scattered individuals together, and then they bring offerings to the physical embodiment of the solar star, appearing as the star of peace. Thus was the religion of peace, of harmony, of universal peace, of human brotherhood, connected cosmically and humanly with the ancient Magi, who laid the best gifts that they had in store for humanity before the cradle of the Son of Man incarnate.

The legend has retained this beautifully, for it says: The Danish king attained an understanding of the Wise Men, of the three Kings, and because he had attained it they bestowed on him their three gifts: first the gift of wisdom, in self-knowledge; secondly, the gift of pious devotion, in self-surrender; and, thirdly, the gift of the victory of life over death, in the power and development of the eternal in the self.

All those who have understood Christianity in this way have seen in it the profound idea in spiritual science of the unification of religions. For they had the first conviction that whoever understands Christianity thus can rise to the highest grade of human development.

1. Ambrogio Borgognone, The Children in the Temple, Basilica of Sant' Ambrogio, Milan

2. Raphael, Madonna del Duca di Terranuova, Staatliche Museen, Berlin

3. The Three Magi, from the Adelphia Sarcophagus, Catacombs of St John, Syracuse, Sicily

4. The Three Magi, St Apollinare Nuovo, Ravenna

PART THREE

Who were the Three Magi?

Having considered the Three Wise Men more generally we will now look at them more as individuals—in so far as this is possible, for over the centuries many legends about them have accrued. Their traditional names of Caspar (a Persian), Melchior (an Indian) and Balthazar (a Babylonian) were mentioned in the previous extract. Caspar also appears as 'Jaspar or Gaspar' and there are variations in the spelling of Balthazar. However, many Syrian Christians name them as Larvandad, Gushnasaph and Hormisdas—all more Persian sounding. Ethiopian Christians have them as Hor, Karsudan and Basanater, and Armenians as Kagpha, Badakharida and Badadilma. There are other variations too, including a Chinese belief that one was Chinese. All these, like their origins, are important for showing that on the whole they come from further east but do not belong to just one nation, race or peoples.

Matthew's Gospel describes them as 'departing to their own country by another way' (2:12). Whether or not the origin of further legends, this 'other way' was indeed circuitous according to some. As we saw previously, one tradition associates them with Cologne—though this seems more to do with their supposed relics or bones. Some of the Uighurs of central Asia are said to claim descent from them, and one interesting legend comes from Provence, where the noble family, the house of Baux, very powerful in medieval times, claimed descent from Balthazar. In Les-Baux-de-Provence their ruined château attracts visitors today and their coat of arms displayed a 16-pointed star in honour of the Magi. Their motto was *A l'asard Bautezar* meaning 'by the grace of Balthazar'. In modern French it became *Au Hasard Balthazar* or 'random Balthazar' and might be better known as the title of a film by Robert Bresson about the life of a long-suffering donkey. In the Middle Ages a knight of the Order of the Temple, Roncelin de Fos was descended from them through his mother, Tiburgette des Baux. He is known for being accused of introducing perverse practices into the Templars' rituals by defendants during the trials of the Templars. His sister Sibylle (Bellette) appears to have married a troubadour, Boniface de Castellane, whose mother was an Alix des Baux.[29] But the family acquired a reputation for misfortune— the German poet Rilke makes a mysterious comment about them in his novel *The Notebooks of Malte Laurids Brigge*.[30]

> Strangers saw him on the Acropolis, and perhaps for many years he was one of the shepherds in Les Baux, and saw petrified time outlast that noble family which, in spite of all their conquests under the holy numbers seven and three, could not overcome the fatal sixteen-rayed star on their own coat-of-arms.

An endnote states:

> . . . They traced their origin to King Balthazar, one of the three wise men of the Gospel, and took for their coat-of-arms the star of Bethlehem. Unfortunately, the star had sixteen rays—an extremely unlucky number, which they tried to counteract by having their possessions in threes and sevens, or multiples of these two lucky numbers.

Their power evidently declined over the centuries and only a few noble families claim descent from them today. Why in view of their exalted heritage they should be perceived as accursed is something of a mystery. Maybe it was because they appropriated the holy star or because of its 'sixteen rays'—some numerologists call 16 a number of 'karmic debt', and Steiner makes a puzzling comment in a lecture given on 16 (!) May 1908[31] that there are '16 ways to perdition' or 16 ways of not advancing or moving forwards in one's incarnations. There may also be an association because of the 16-petalled lotus flower or chakra in the region of the throat which is linked with the planet Mars.

All this may be something of a digression, so let us now look at earlier possible incarnations of the Three Wise Men. In the first of the following extracts we are reminded of the destiny of the Jewish people in preparing for the birth of Jesus, and of the incarnation of Zarathustra in Babylon, where, during the 'Babylonian captivity' of the Hebrews, prominent leaders came into contact with him. In the next, albeit short account, we learn that the reborn Zarathustra was also the teacher of Pythagoras who was in Babylon at that time, and that he moreover reincarnated as one of the Three Wise Men. It is known that the famous Greek mathematician and spiritual teacher was captured and taken to Babylon in 525 BC, so it would have been during this time that he became a pupil of Zaratas (Zarathustra).

The former identities of the other two Magi have not apparently been made known to us, but a good case is made for one having been the prophet Daniel. He was taken to Babylon in 605 BC when very young. According to the Old Testament Book of Daniel, King Nebuchadnezzar besieged Jerusalem, destroyed the Temple and took many Hebrews captive. Daniel's skills and powers of interpreting dreams were recognized after many trials and he was eventually honoured by the king. He was renamed by a chief eunuch as Belteshazzar, meaning 'protect his life' (Dan. 1:7), which later became rendered as Balthazar. Thus he already bore one of the traditional names of the three Magi. Daniel reached a high political position in the courts of successive Babylonian kings, and then came the dramatic incident as described in the Book of Daniel, a scene so wonderfully painted by Rembrandt, when at King Belshazzar's feast a mysterious hand appears and writes on the wall, *mene, mene, tekel, parsin,* which Daniel interprets as 'God has numbered the days of your kingdom and brought it to an end; you have been weighed in the balances and found wanting; your kingdom is divided and given to the Medes and Persians (Dan. 5:24–8). And according to the chronicle, King Darius the Mede invaded that night, slew Belshazzar and became king in his place.

The problem here is that historians state it was the Persian King Cyrus the Great who invaded Babylon in 539 BC, overcoming Belshazzar, and a year later released the Jews from their captivity, allowing them to return to Judaea and rebuild the Temple. Darius reigned from 522 to 486 BC, which means Daniel must have lived until at least 520 BC and reached the age of 97 if they were to have overlapped. Thus Emil Bock considers that events were 'veiled' and Daniel as a highly placed statesman already knew King Cyrus and prepared for his taking over the Babylonian kingdom before he actually invaded, and that there was another Darius of the Medes who lived at the time of Cyrus, who favoured Daniel in some way. He suggests this is expressed in the Bible as: 'So this Daniel prospered during the reign of Darius [at the Median court] and the reign of Cyrus the Persian(Dan. 6:28).[32] The reason for a preoccupation with these events is in order to see whether a third significant figure can be identified as a previous incarnation of one of the Magi and pupil of Zaratas. Hans Gsänger[33] suggests King Cyrus as a likely candidate as he was certainly in Babylon from 539 to 538 at the same time as Daniel. Pythagoras arrived in 525 and Zaratas lived there from 599 to 522, so all three could have been his pupils. Erwin Horstmann[34] points out that 'Melchior' is a Hebrew name meaning 'king of light', a fitting reference to Cyrus who adhered to Zarathustra's religion of light and also knew something of the mission of the Jews. Bock describes him as 'the embodiment of an ideal ruler'. 'Caspar' is a Persian word meaning 'treasurer'—one who has to keep accounts, a possible hint at the mathematician Pythagoras.[35]

M.J.

10. Munich, 7 December 1909

We must now show how the Hebrews gradually developed from generation to generation so that finally the body of Jesus could be produced, and the ancient Hebrew stream flow into Christianity . . . The life of an individual can be divided into periods of seven years. The first period, in which the physical body simply builds its forms, extends from birth to the change of teeth at the age of seven. The second period, in which the etheric body is active in growth and forming, continues until puberty. The forms are defined until the age of seven and the already defined forms are then enlarged. From 14 to 21 the astral body is especially predominant, and at 21 the true I is born and becomes independent. The life of the individual runs its course in certain periods until the birth of the human I.

In the same way, the gifts of the people that was to provide a body for the most perfect I had to develop gradually. What takes place over years in an individual, however, develops in a people over generations. Each successive generation must further develop the characteristics of the preceding one. To explain the occult reasons for this would lead us too far afield, but you might recall a quite ordinary phenomenon. Just remember that certain qualities are inherited not directly, but skip a generation. For example, it is the grandson who resembles the grandfather in those characteristics. It was the same in the inheritance of qualities in successive generations of the Hebrews; every other generation was skipped.

What is one period of seven years in an individual's life

corresponds in the successive generations of a people to two periods or 14 generations. We can therefore say the Hebrews developed in twice seven or 14 generations, which corresponds to the period from birth to the change of teeth in the individual. The following period corresponds to that between the change of teeth and puberty and again comprises twice seven generations. A third period of twice seven generations corresponds to the years between 14 and 21, when the astral body is especially prominent. It was then possible for the I to be born in the Hebrew people after three times twice seven or three times 14, that is, 42 generations.

To describe the body that became Zarathustra's instrument, I had to show how the seed given to Abraham developed through thrice 14 generations so that the I could be born, just as in the individual the I is born into the threefold corporeality after thrice seven years. The writer of St Matthew's Gospel shows this. He describes thrice 14 generations—the generations from Abraham to David, from David to the Babylonian captivity, and from the Babylonian captivity to the birth of Jesus. Here, from the profundity of knowledge St Matthew's Gospel points to the mission of the Hebrews, showing how the forces were gradually developed that made it possible for the perfect I attained by Zarathustra to be born in a body produced by this people.

Looking at the destiny of the Hebrews, we find that the Babylonian captivity occurred at the period when the individual, after the age of 14, prepares for life, when the hopes of youth to be realized later take root. The Babylonian captivity was the time when the astral body of the Hebrews developed, and what gives this astral body its impulse in the final 14 generations of the 42 was implanted into it then. That is why the Hebrews were led into the Babylonian captivity, where, six hundred years before our era, Zarathas or Nazarathos was incarnated as the teacher in the mystery schools of the Babylonians. There, the most prominent Hebrew leaders came in contact with Zarathas, the great teacher of that era. Zarathas joined them and became their teacher. From him the Hebrew leaders received the impulse that, in their last 14 generations, prepared them for the birth of Jesus.

History as we know it then unfolded, and we see the writer of St Matthew's Gospel take into account a law in the spiritual sphere that will be recognized more and more as significant for all life. This is the law that whatever has happened earlier is repeated at a higher stage. This is expressed in science in a somewhat distorted form in the axiom that what occurs at a lower stage of the species throughout long epochs is repeated in brief in each individual. The writer of St Matthew's Gospel shows this in a magnificent way by saying that the I of Zarathustra was to incarnate in a body that was gradually developed within the Abrahamic people.

Abraham proceeded from Ur in Chaldea, the place where Babylonian civilization originated, through Asia Minor to Palestine. Through the dreams of Joseph, his descendants were led farther south to Egypt and, after they had received the Egyptian impulse, they returned to Canaan. This was the fate of the whole people. First, they were led through Canaan to Egypt, and then back again to Canaan. This fate of the whole people was to be repeated in brief. After all that had originated in Abraham had been developed, after the sheaths had been prepared, Zarathustra's I again took Chaldea as its point of departure. His spirit was connected with Chaldea, and in his last incarnation he was the mystery teacher there.

What path does Zarathustra's soul take when it incarnates in Bethlehem? He had remained connected with the Magi, who had been initiated in the Chaldean mystery schools. They remembered that they had heard him say he would reappear and that his soul, which had always been called 'the golden star', would proceed at a particular time to Bethlehem. When the time came, they followed the path his soul took, thus repeating the path of the Old Testament Hebrews. As Abraham travelled the road to Canaan, so this star, the soul of Zarathustra, also followed it. The three Magi followed the star of Zarathustra, and he led them to the place where he was born into the body from the Abrahamic people that was destined for him. Thus, the I of Zarathustra repeated in spirit the path Abraham had taken to Palestine.

The Old Testament Hebrews then had to seek the way to Egypt. They were led there by Joseph's dreams. Now the I that was born in the Jesus child of Bethlehem was led through the dreams of another Joseph to Egypt along the same path the Abrahamic people had followed earlier. Zarathustra's I repeated in Jesus' body the ancient Hebrew's destiny, going first to Egypt and then returning to Palestine. Here, we have a recapitulation in spirit through the I of Zarathustra, reflecting the earlier fate of the Hebrews.

11. Budapest, 31 May 1909

Ahura Mazda himself, the Leader of the Sun, had to descend to earth to bring light into this icy separateness [of souls who were cut off from the true spiritual world]. He had to become a human being in the physical world in order to help both the living and the dead. He had to be a human among humans! The high and the magnificent that lives in the sun descended to earth and revealed itself in and to humanity. Previously, it had revealed itself in the elements, for example to Moses in the fire of the burning bush and in the lightning of Sinai. The Israelites were to make no graven image of their God. Why? Because no external name can be given to 'Me', the Divine Being; only an entirely different name can express the 'I am the I am!' The only possibility of discovering the Spirit of the Sun's name is to seek it in the human being. That which lives as I in human beings is the Christ Being.

The Jehovah revelation precedes the Christ. That was at the time when the Christ Being could gradually descend to the earth. What had Zarathustra once vowed to the high Sun Being? What sacrifices did he want to make to him? His body, senses, life, and speech. Zarathustra was reincarnated as a contemporary of the great Buddha. He could then build up the etheric and astral bodies that he had sacrificed. He was reborn as Zarathas or Nazarathos, and he became the teacher of Pythagoras, who himself was reincarnated as one of the Three Wise Men of the East and became one of the disciples of Jesus of Nazareth. Zarathustra, who had once sacrificed his etheric and astral bodies, was also able to give up his external sheath to Him whose coming he had once announced. As the Jesus of Nazareth of western occultism, he could place his physical body at the disposal of the Sun Spirit and was then able to say, 'I am the Light of the World!'

What Became of the Three Wise Men?

If the preceding account bears some truth then it is hardly surprising that the Three Wise Men went on to become even more remarkable figures within religious and esoteric history. An early Lesson from Steiner's first Esoteric School has the title 'The Connection of the Masters with the Raising of the Dead in the Gospels',[36] written down as notes after the Lesson was heard by Elisabeth Vreede. The English typescript translation included the words that a note in her handwriting was added to the title, 'What became of the Three Wise Men from the East?'[37] Lest it seem too far-fetched that the three Magi could have reincarnated so quickly as to be young people living at the time of Christ, if we look back to the extract stating that Pythagoras had been one of the three Magi we will see added the words 'and became one of the disciples of Jesus of Nazareth'. The German word here is *Schüler* which can also be translated as 'pupil'.

The Lesson is remarkable in that it succinctly conveys so much. Three 'raisings' are described: the Youth of Nain (Luke 7:11–17), Lazarus (John 11:1–44), and the daughter of Jairus (Matthew 9:18–26; Mark 5:22–43; Luke 8:40–56). Andrew Welburn has pointed out that the expression to be 'raised up' was to be found in many of the ancient mysteries: 'the initiate was raised from a prone state (symbolically death and/or infancy) by the hierophant: the Christian Father Tertullian calls this a picture of (the) resurrection'.[38] Thus three potential initiates arise from apparent death. Two become well known and one not at all. The Youth of Nain reincarnates as Mani, the founder of Manichaeism—here Rudolf Steiner recounts a more legendary version of his youth, but put briefly his story is more usually described as follows. It is generally accepted that he was born on 14 April AD 216 in Babylon (Iraq) and probably grew up within a Gnostic Jewish-Christian sect, the Elchasaites. Aged 12, he received a revelation from a being he called 'the Twin'—his higher, angelic self, who reappeared when he was 24, sending him out into the world with his newly found understanding. Having been known as Kurkabios, he took the name Mani (Greek: Manes), meaning Manas-bearer, or bearer of the Spirit Self, the next higher stage of human consciousness towards which we are evolving. He gathered followers and his teaching spread across Asia to the Far East, including China and probably Japan. Initially supported in this by King Shapur I of Persia, he later fell foul of the latter's descendant Barham and the Zoroastrian priesthood. He was imprisoned as a traitor, tortured and died in prison aged 60 in AD 277. His teaching is mainly concerned with the *problem of evil.* He described evil as having come into the world at the same time as good, as light and darkness; elaborate myths show evil's assault on good, but ultimately it must be rescued and redeemed, because of there existing 'light' within every living being. This will only be possible in a future epoch but preparations must be made much sooner. We learn that Mani then reincarnated as the historical figure behind Parzival. In Wolfram von Eschenbach's version of the story, Parzival does not claim the right to be king of the Holy Grail until he has brought his half-brother Feirefis, a Muslim, to the Grail castle. As Parzival this individuality is particularly significant for the fifth—current—epoch of evolution, which is a kind of mirror of the third, the Egyptian period. He embodies the ordinary person struggling to develop from foolishness, through doubt, to blessedness.

Rudolf Steiner significantly pointed out as early as 1902[39] that Lazarus, after being raised from apparent death, became 'the disciple whom Jesus loved' and the author of St John's Gospel, Letters of John and the Book of Revelation. Other scholars, too, have made this suggestion or at least part of it.[40] In the extracts from conversations following this, Steiner goes further in stating that Lazarus-John reincarnated as Christian Rosenkreutz, the founder of the Rosicrucian Brotherhood in the Middle Ages, and later in the eighteenth century as the Count of Saint-Germain. He becomes a guiding figure within esoteric Christianity and a leading master of the West.[41]

Of Jairus' daughter, sadly nothing more has so far come to light. This need not be taken to be because she was 'only a woman'—Steiner often stressed the importance of female incarnations from our time onwards. The fact of the knowledge of her 'raising' coming to light in our time seems to indicate this. As a representative of a future epoch, the seventh, it seems probable that her true mission is a future one. Steiner also made the connection of her 'raising' with the preceding event of the healing of the woman with constant bleeding who touches his garment. She released too much blood, but the girl could not reach puberty and start to bleed. A karmic connection was between the two, but also, through Christ, an exchange of energies became possible—a deed that human beings may be able to perform consciously in the future.

Catacomb paintings and sculptures on early Christian sarcophagi often depict the Magi, and frequently the 'raisings' as mentioned are shown too, with Christ holding a hierophant's 'wand'.[42] The first Christians seemed to be aware of the initiatory aspect of these—and possibly even their connection with the Magi. Such aspects are gradually coming to light once more.

This Lesson has been included in its entirety because of its special nature. The references to further healings in the Gospels are something that can be left to ponder on.

M.J.

12a. Esoteric Lesson, possibly Karlsruhe, 21 or 23 January 1911

Matthew's Gospel tells us how three Magi came from the East bringing their incense, gold and myrrh to the newborn Jesus child, the reincarnated Zarathustra. They pay homage to their reborn master, who, in his various incarnations, had been active in the past three cultural epochs. They are at the same time the guardians of the ancient store of wisdom from the Old Indian, the Old Persian and the Egypto-Babylonian epochs. And by laying this in the symbolic form of incense, gold and myrrh at the feet of the Jesus Child they also demonstrate what was active in those epochs as a germ of future cultures that can be rescued for the future of humankind only through being penetrated by the power of Christ, which would one day ensoul this child. They themselves would not experience the rebirth of the wisdom of their cultural epochs. 'They departed into their own country another way.'

But we can ask ourselves the following question: 'Where did these Three Wise Men subsequently stay? What will become of their wisdom?' And we should remind ourselves that cultures rising and passing away here on earth bear a seed that can be fructified by the Christ-impulse, and will come to a new blossoming in the epochs following the Mystery of Golgotha. What was offered to the Jesus child by the Three Magi from the East as the germ of a new culture will be reawakened by Christ. It contains the forces that will truly permeate these later epochs with the Christ Spirit. Everything pertaining to the store of wisdom contained in the third post-Atlantean epoch will be reawakened by the Christ to fructify our fifth epoch. The second epoch—that of Zarathustra—will be reawakened to being a true understanding of the Christ in the sixth epoch. And the first epoch—the Ancient Indian epoch—will experience a reawakening in the seventh epoch with the help of the Christ-power.

And in every instance Christ must be the Awakener of a *particular* individual, a human soul whose destiny it is to be chosen as the special vehicle to convey this seed of culture from ancient times, and who, at the same time, is the soul best suited to ensure that what has been brought to humankind as a gift by Christ will be led on into the future, so that the understanding of Christ and for his mission may also be imparted to future ages of humankind.

We shall now consider these awakenings one after another.

FIRST: In St Luke's Gospel (chapter 7) the awakening of the Young Man of Nain is described to us in stirring words. Every word is important in this account, which indicates that in the Young Man of Nain lives all of the third epoch—the Egypto-Chaldean cultural epoch—as it was able to develop under the influence of those powers then active.

The Young Man of Nain of St Luke's Gospel is no other than the Young Man of Sais—the difference in the spiritual background of the third and fourth cultural epochs is hidden in the very name. The Young Man of Sais wanted to delve into the secrets of the world without preparation; he wanted to be like the other initiates, a 'Son of the Widow' Isis, who mourned her lost husband, Osiris. But because he was not prepared, because he wanted to unveil the statue of Isis himself here on the physical plane and glimpse the heavenly secrets, he died. No human mortal could at *that* time lift the veil of Isis. The powerlessness of the Egyptian wisdom is symbolized in the Young Man of Sais.

Again, he was born and grew up as the Young Man of Nain. Again he was the 'Son of the Widow'. Again he died in his youth. And Christ approached as the dead one was carried out through the city gates. And 'many people of the city were with her' (his mother). It was the host of the Egyptian initiates, all of them dead, who bury the dead. 'And when the Lord saw her he had compassion on her.' He felt compassion for the mother, who stood there in the manner of Isis, the sister and wife of Osiris. And He spoke: 'Young Man, I say to you, Arise! And he who was dead sat up and began to speak. And He delivered him to his mother.' The former Isis has descended to earth. Her powers can be experienced even here on earth. The son has been given back to his mother and it now rests with him to unite himself completely with her. 'And those who were present glorified God saying: A great prophet is risen up among us.' For, through the kind of initiation represented in this awakening, the Christ had sown a seed that will only come to blossom in the young man's next life on earth.

A great prophet, a great religious teacher, has developed in the Young Man of Nain! In the third century AD Mani, or Manes, the founder of Manichaeism, made his appearance in Babylon. A strange legend relates the following story about him.

Skythianos and Terebinthus—or Buddha—were his predecessors. The latter was the pupil of the former. After the violent death of Skythianos, Terebinthus took the books of Skythianos and fled with them to Babylon. It went badly with him too; only one old widow accepted his teaching. She inherited his books and left them to her foster child—a boy of twelve years, whom she adopted when he was seven years old (as a slave) in place of her own son. Her adopted son, who can also be called the 'Son of a Widow', appeared at the age of 24 as Manes, the founder of Manichaeism.

In his teachings all the wisdom of the ancient religions is gathered together and illumined by him with a Christian gnosticism that enabled the devotees of the Egypto-Babylonian star wisdom, the followers of the ancient Persian religion—even the Buddhists of India—to absorb an understanding of the Christ-impulse in this form.

This soul that formerly lived in the Young Man of Nain was engaged in preparation; he was initiated in this way by Christ for a future when the contents of Manichaeism, which have not yet fully developed, will arise for the salvation of the people of the ancient East. During his life as Manes this soul worked to prepare for his real future mission: to bring about the true reconciliation of all religions.

To achieve this he had to be born again as a soul with a very special relationship to the Christ. All that had arisen in this soul as ancient and new knowledge during its lifetime as Manes had to become submerged again. As the 'innocent fool' it inevitably had to confront the external knowledge of the world and the working of Christ in the depths of its being. He was born again as Parzival, the son of Herzeleide, the tragic personality deserted by her husband. As the son of this widow, Parzival again left his mother and set out into the world. After straying in many different directions he succeeded in being chosen as the Guardian of the Holy Grail. And the continuation of the Parzival legend tells us how he again set out towards the East, how he discovered his brother among the people of the dark race, and how these people will one day also receive the blessings from the Holy Grail. Thus he prepared himself in his life as Parzival to become a future teacher of Christianity, whose task it will be to penetrate Christianity itself more and more with the teachings of karma and reincarnation when the time is ripe.

SECOND: The second post-Atlantean epoch was that of Zarathustra. This has a special connection to Christ, because Zarathustra directed people's attention to Ahura Mazda, the Sun God, who was drawing nearer to earth, and was none other than the future Jesus [Christ]. And the whole mission of Zarathustra was to prepare the way for Christ by teaching people to work for and value the world, and not flee from evil, but to conquer and redeem it. And so the individuality of Zarathustra, the most highly developed human entelechy, was fit to be chosen to dwell for 18[43] years within the sheaths that were later to take up the Christ. His I withdrew from these sheaths shortly before the Baptism by John in the Jordan. So it was that he was not present in the flesh as Christ walked the earth. He himself took up incarnation very soon after leaving the three sheaths of the Nathan Jesus. His I united with the etheric body of the Solomon Jesus, which, at the latter's death, had been taken up into the spiritual world by the mother of the Nathanic Jesus.

Therefore it was not possible for Christ Jesus to choose Zarathustra as the representative of the second post-Atlantean epoch when the raising from death took place; but there was living at that time another individuality whose development and the importance of whose mission for humanity ran strangely parallel to that of Zarathustra. This was Lazarus, the reincarnated Hiram Abiff,[44] the most important of the Sons of Cain, who had similarly worked upon his earthly mission out of the forces of the I, just as Zarathustra had done in Ancient Persia. He became 'ill' and 'died' and was laid in the grave. Christ Jesus heard of his illness and spoke to His Disciples of Lazarus' death. 'Then spoke Thomas, called the Twin, to the other Disciples: Let us go that we may die with him' (John 11:16).

In this awakening Lazarus was to undergo, Thomas, the 'Twin', represented the souls belonging to the second post-Atlantean epoch—just as at the awakening of the Young Man of Nain the 'people of the city' represented the third post-Atlantean epoch. The second post-Atlantean epoch was the epoch of the Twins. The words of Thomas, which are otherwise completely incomprehensible, signify that the second post-Atlantean epoch is willing to be awakened by Christ. What lived as a seed of culture in the Ancient Persian epoch is *not* dead. It is *not* a matter of the awakening of a dead person, but of the initiation of someone who is alive. That is the great difference in the account of this awakening and that of the other two. Therefore Christ spoke the words: 'I am the Resurrection and the Life, he that believeth in me, though he were dead, yet shall he live.'

And Christ Jesus approached the grave in which the supposed dead man had been placed and spoke the sacramental words before the crowds: 'Lazarus come forth!' And he that was dead came forth, bound hand and foot with grave clothes and his face bound about with a napkin. And Christ Jesus spoke the words—at the same time indicating that from this time on this initiate would commence his task: 'Loosen him and let him go.'

He is not a youth, like the Young Man of Nain—he is a man in the full possession of his spiritual powers. The awakened Lazarus is the one who wrote the St John's Gospel. He is the one who stood beneath the Cross and to whom Christ Jesus spoke from the Cross, indicating the Mother

The Raising of Jairus's Daughter, the Adelphia Sarcophagus, Catacombs of St John, Syracuse, Sicily

Sophia-Mary: 'Behold thy mother!' So, proclaimed once more is his strange vicarious relationship to the I of Zarathustra who, as the Solomon Jesus child, was really born as the son of this mother.

Endowed with this strength he can already unfold his activity before the sixth post-Atlantean epoch. Even during the fifth cultural epoch he is making preparation for the sixth, which is that epoch that is to reveal the deepest understanding for the Christ-impulse and which will best understand the Gospel of St John.

(Among the twelve Apostles Lazarus-John is similarly also represented by another. John, the brother of James and the son of Zebedee, is not an Apostle in the real sense. James and John are in a way a single person. They represent, in the intimate circle around Christ, the powers of the intellectual or mind soul, which plays a dual role in the human being but is nevertheless a unity. That is why these two are called 'Sons of Thunder', for thunder is in the outer world what thought is for the inner life of human beings. But when Lazarus becomes John, he takes the place of the one who is Zebedee's son, and as such he is the one who lay on the breast of Jesus at the Last Supper.)

THIRD: When Christ Jesus walked the earth only the last dwindling descendants remained of the third post-Atlantean epoch. The second cultural epoch had almost entirely disappeared as a bearer of civilization, and only a few of the adherents of the largely degenerate Zarathustra religion could still be found scattered here and there. But the first epoch—the Ancient Indian cultural epoch—the oldest and most spiritual of them all, had successors, both at the time of Christ Jesus and during our own epoch, even though it had become degenerate by being infected with materialism. This epoch will be the last to be renewed, the one that will have to wait longest.

This awakening is mysteriously revealed in the story of the raising of the twelve-year-old daughter of Jairus and in the preceding account of the healing of the woman who had suffered for twelve years from an issue of blood (Luke 8:40–56). The girl is very near death when Christ comes to heal her. But the woman is there too whose illness started at the birth of this child. The blood, which is the life force, flows from her. She typifies the once-flourishing spiritual culture of Ancient India, which cannot be healed by any doctor—for no yoga methods, no Vedanta philosophy, however sublime, can rescue the Indian cultural epoch from destruction.

The woman is karmically related to this girl who has reached the age of twelve years. That means that the development of the etheric body is coming to an end. The Ancient Indian cultural epoch was when the etheric body was being developed. What was sown as a seed in the etheric body during the Ancient Indian epoch will be quickened to life and preserved for the last, the seventh epoch.

But this awakening can only take place when the woman has been healed. This woman approached Christ from the crowd, 'from behind' (Luke 8:44), touched the border of His garment and was healed; for 'your faith has made you whole'

(Luke 8:48; Mark 5:4). She was healed because she had a faith within herself that the spirit is incarnated on earth. And after she was healed of the issue of blood through her free decision to touch Christ's garment, what was once within her as a living force and is beginning to die—and could even be regarded as dead—could be brought to life again: it is the daughter of Jairus, the 'ruler of the synagogue', for the first cultural epoch was that of the Brahmins, the priests. There was a great multitude about the dead girl 'that wept and wailed greatly'—again, it was those belonging to the first post-Atlantean epoch who were bewailing what was past. St Matthew alludes to the 'pipers' (minstrels) (Matthew 9:23) who played beside the dead. Krishna also played upon the pipe and the people followed the sound of it.

Christ Jesus, however, evicted them all. A great mystery is about to unfold, for the awakening to life of just this first cultural epoch, connected with the development of the etheric body, is related to the deep secrets of human nature. Jesus takes with him only Peter, John, and James, and the father and mother of the child. All together, with Christ and the child herself, there were thus seven people present: the three Spirit Powers, the three Soul Powers, and Christ as the Cosmic I. Thus the epoch of the ancient Holy Rishis was mirrored in these seven people. Just as the Rishis could only function when all seven of them were present, so could the maiden only be raised from the dead when the sevenfold powers were gathered together. And she was healed and Christ Jesus commanded that she should be given something to eat. For the Ancient Indian civilization had previously not needed to 'eat', it had received its knowledge directly from the spiritual world through the wonderful development of the etheric body alone. But this source of nourishment had come to an end. From now on the people inevitably had to eat what could be supplied from their surroundings. And Christ Jesus 'charged them directly that no one should know it', a command that it is impossible to interpret in the sense of a physical reality. But the secrets that were enacted in this resurrection must remain hidden and unknown for a long time to come.

Alongside these three awakenings belonging to the three pre-Christian epochs, several strange accounts from the Gospels can be connected with the entering of the Christ-impulse into humanity's development.

FOURTH: In St John's Gospel (4:47–54) we are told of the nobleman's son—that is the son of the Roman—who was at the point of death. Portrayed in him is the languishing of the fourth post-Atlantean epoch, the Graeco-Roman period. Christ healed him because of the father's plea, because the father believed even without 'signs and wonders'. The son was not raised from the dead, for he had not died. The fourth post-Atlantean epoch was still living at the time of Christ Jesus; it was merely ill and could be healed only through faith. For only in the form of faith could the Graeco-Roman epoch take the Christ power into itself.

FIFTH: The account of the healing of the sick man at Bethesda, the pool with the five porches, immediately follows this account in St John's Gospel. These indicate the fifth post-Atlanean epoch with all that lives within it of the forces of the previous epoch. The people lying there are ill. They do not have the right attitude towards the spiritual world, and have sunk too deeply into matter. From time to time an angel descends and moves the water. A fresh revelation from the spiritual worlds heals those nearest to it, but it does not cure those who come later. And so there was a man there who had waited for 38 years without being able to get near the water. Thirty-eight is twice 19, which is the time it takes for Sun, Moon and Earth to return to the same relative positions to one another—or in other words, it is the time it takes a human being's thinking, feeling and willing to go through all possible phases in their relationship to one another. Thus the period of 19 years represents a *single* earth life, and the 38 years denote two incarnations, which is about the average number of lives human beings have experienced since the coming of Christ, and brings us to our own day, when a new revelation of Christ will be revealed out of the spiritual world. Christ Jesus did not heal this man by lowering him into the pool when the angel appeared, but said to him: 'Rise, take up your bed, and walk!' That is to say, He strengthens in human beings the power that can overcome illness. But the man did not know who had healed him, 'for Christ had vanished from sight, a multitude being in that place' (John 5:13). Christ had indeed been active within him, but the man knew nothing about it in his ordinary consciousness. Thus it has been since the Mystery of Golgotha, right up to our own time. But afterwards 'Jesus found him in the temple' and 'the man departed and told the Jews that it was Jesus who had made him a whole'.

Now he knew that the word is true that Christ Jesus spoke to the Jews: 'My Father has worked until now, and now I work.' And again Christ said: 'The hour is coming, and now is, when the dead shall hear the voice of the Son of God; and they that hear shall live,' the hour that will strike in our presence, the hour when Christ will come to judge the dead and become the Lord of Destiny. Thus in many ways this account of the healing of the sick man of Bethesda bears reference to our own time.

SIXTH: In St Luke's Gospel a parable that points to the spiritual situation of the sixth post-Atlantean epoch has been secretly introduced. As we have seen, this epoch, which signifies the reawakening of the second post-Atlantean epoch, is prepared by Christ Jesus through the raising of Lazarus. And in St Luke's Gospel, Christ Jesus related a parable just after having spoken about good and evil, and about 'the servants of God and the servants of Mammon'. In the sixteenth chapter He told of a certain poor man named Lazarus who had, while on earth, had a bad time, but after his death he was received into Abraham's bosom—whereas the rich man, who had fared sumptuously on earth, was received into hell.

So will the good and the bad split off from one another in the sixth cultural epoch, and the true picture of events is staged in the spiritual world. The naming of the poor man connected the parable to Lazarus of St John's Gospel; and the sixth post-Atlantean epoch is expressed in the figure of the rich man, who says, 'I have five brethren' still unconverted. They represent that part of humanity that has not taken the Christ into itself in the sixth epoch, and so must succumb to the evil forces.

SEVENTH: The seventh cultural epoch is not mentioned again specifically, since this has already been given in the relationship existing between the woman with the issue of blood and the twelve-year-old girl. The woman has already been healed when the maiden is restored to life. The one event cannot take place without the other.

In this and other ways the Gospel writers have secretly introduced into their writings the course of the historical development of humankind.[45]

From Conversations with Rudolf Steiner

In the following conversations, the 'Master Jesus' is referred to. This individuality is none other than the reincarnated Zarathustra, who, after incarnating in the Matthew Jesus child, continues to reincarnate and bears the title Master Jesus as distinct from Christ, the purely spiritual being. He becomes a guiding being for esoteric Christianity and was designated as the leading Master of the West alongside Christian Rosenkreutz.[46] He is said to have taught the Gnostics[47] (we do not know under what name) and later appears as the 'Friend of God from the Highlands' who visited Johannes Tauler and his companions in the late fourteenth century. There is also a beautiful legend that at every Eastertide he visits the place of the Mystery of Golgotha—whether or not he is actually incarnated. In a lecture from 1912 Steiner speaks as if this is more than just a legend: 'For while sects of different kinds scattered over the earth are at strife among themselves, he through whom the greatest of all tidings of peace was brought to the earth looks again at the places that were the scene of his earthly deeds.'[48] He continues to guide souls towards the next epoch, the sixth or Aquarian age of brotherly love.

Thus we have come in a full circle. It appears in this account that he is brought together with his pupils, the Three Wise Men, to behold the greatest Mystery. But to attribute further the identities of the three with what has been given about possible incarnations would be to indulge in speculation and is best left to the reader to consider.

M.J.

12b. Notes from personal conversations with Rudolf Steiner regarding the Master Jesus and Christian Rosenkreutz

Rudolf Steiner replied to a question concerning the Friend of God from the Highlands that he was the Master Jesus who, since the Mystery of Golgotha, has incarnated during every century. To another question about whether he was currently incarnated, Rudolf Steiner said that he was living at the time in the Carpathians, and indicated that they were in spiritual contact.

(Recorded by Friedrich Rittelmeyer, no date)

To a question about the significance of the assembly of twelve leading Friends of God with their aged leader (the 'Friend of God from the Highlands') as described in the leader's last letter, written at Easter 1380, Rudolf Steiner replied: 'You see, this is where you have the change to Rosicrucianism. It is the same thing that is pointed to in "The Mysteries", a Christmas and Easter poem by Goethe.' Since that time Christian Rosenkreutz has become the leading personality in the spiritual life of the West. Both he and the Master Jesus, the Friend of God from the Highlands, have been incarnated in every century since then. They incarnate in turns every century, and from that time on the Master Jesus has worked along with Christian Rosenkreutz.

(Recorded by Wilhelm Rath from his conversation with Rudolf Steiner in Stuttgart, 16 October 1922)

To the question as to whether the Friend of God from the Highlands was Christian Rosenkreutz, Rudolf Steiner replied: 'No! But Christian Rosenkreutz was among the twelve Friends of God whose secret meeting was reported by the Friend of God from the Highlands.' To the further question as to whether the Friend of God was Zarathustra, Rudolf Steiner answered 'Yes.'

To the question: Is he who is called John in the first three Gospels the same as Lazarus? Rudolf Steiner answered: 'The writer of Saint John's Gospel is Lazarus. He is only called "John" in the same way that many were called "John" in his day.'...

(Recorded conversations of the Christian Community priests Werner Klein and Emil Bock with Rudolf Steiner, February 1924)

...The Master Jesus is in continual incarnation, with intervals that never exceed twelve years.

(Recorded by Emmy von Gummppenberg, no date)

With Regard to Mani

The Young Man of Nain became a pupil and follower of Christ after he had been raised from the dead. He did not belong to the Twelve.

Question: Is he not named as a pupil of Christ in the apocryphal Gospels?

Answer: 'In his following incarnation he was Mani. His further incarnations can be recognized by legends similar to that of the Lazarus awakening.'

(Recorded from conversations of the Christian Community priests Werner Klein and Emil Bock with Rudolf Steiner, February 1924)

Mani will not incarnate during this century, but intends to do so in the next century, if he can find a suitable body. The ordinary kind of education does not provide any possibility for Mani to develop; only Waldorf education would do so. If the right conditions are provided he will appear as a teacher of humankind and take up leadership in matters of art and religion. He will act from the power of the Grail Mysteries, and he will instruct humankind so that they may decide even about good and evil.

(Recorded by Ehrenfried Pfeiffer from his conversation with Rudolf Steiner between 1919 and 1921)

Sources of Extracts

1. *From Jesus to Christ*, lecture, Karlsruhe 12 October 1911, GA 131, Rudolf Steiner Press, 1991
2. *The Gospel of St Luke,* lecture, Basel 18 September 1909, GA 114, Rudolf Steiner Press, 1975
3. *The Gospel of St Luke*, lecture, 19 September 1909, see above
4. *The Gospel of St Matthew*, lecture, Bern 6 September 1910, GA 123, Rudolf Steiner Press, 1965
5. *Universal Spirituality and Human Physicality,* lecture, Basel, 23 December 1920, GA 202, Rudolf Steiner Press, 2014
6. *Turning Points in Spiritual History: Zarathustra*, lecture, Berlin 19 January 1911, GA 60, Garber Communications Inc: Spiritual Science Library, 1987
7. *The Gospel of St Matthew*, lecture, Bern 6 September 1910, GA 123, Rudolf Steiner Press, 1965
8. *The Festivals and Their Meaning: Christmas,* lecture, Berlin 30 December 1904, 'On the Three Magi', *Nachricht*: 1942/19:1, Rudolf Steiner Press, 1996
9. *The Mysteries*, lecture, Cologne 25 December 1907, GA 98, Rudolf Steiner Publishing Co., 1946. See also in *The Secret Stream*, Anthroposophic Press, 2000
10. *The Universal Human*, lecture, Munich 7 December 1909, GA 117, Anthroposophic Press, 1990
11. *The Principle of Spiritual Economy*, Budapest, 31 May 1909, GA 109, Anthroposophic Press/Rudolf Steiner Press, 1986

12a. *From the History and Contents of the First Section of the Esoteric School 1904–1914*, GA 264, Esoteric Lesson, possibly Karlsruhe 21 or 23 January 1911, Anthroposophic Press, 1998

12b. See above

Notes

A good general account of the Magi and their legends can be found on the Wikipedia website under 'Biblical Magi'.

1. Ormond Edwards, *The Time of Christ. A Chronology of the Incarnation*, Floris Books, Edinburgh 1986.
2. See David Ovason, *The Two Children. A Study of the Two Jesus Children in Literature and Art*, Century, London 2001/Floris, Lindisfarne Books, 2011.
3. Painted because of the prophetic verse from Isaiah 1:3, 'The ox knows its owner, and the ass its master's crib, but Israel does not know, my people does not understand.'
4. See for instance lecture, Berlin 24 April 1917, in *Building Stones for an Understanding of the Mystery of Golgotha*, GA/CW 175, Rudolf Steiner Press, 2015.
5. This is distinct from the Coptic Sethian Gnostic Gospel in *The Nag Hammadi Library*, Brill 1988.
6. *The Apocryphal New Testament*, p. 11, translated by Montague Rhodes James, Clarendon Press, Oxford 1972.
7. Version taken from above, p. 66.
8. Geza Vermes, *The Complete Dead Sea Scrolls in English*, revised edition Penguin Books, 2011 (p. 86, p. 161).
9. *The Gospel of St Matthew*, GA 123, lecture, Bern 4 September 1910, Rudolf Steiner Press, 1965.
10. Emil Bock, *The Childhood of Jesus. The Unknown Years.* Floris Books, Edinburgh 1980.
11. See *Occult Science. An Outline/An Outline of Esoteric Science*, GA 13, Rudolf Steiner Press, 2011/Anthroposophic Press, Hudson, NY 1997, for an explanation of these evolutionary periods.

12. See *The Spiritual Hierarchies in the Physical World*, GA 110, Anthroposophic Press, Hudson, NY 1996, for a fuller description of these spirits.
13. The spiritual chronicle of all events.
14. Apparently never named.
15. This Buddhist term usually refers to the 'manifest body', the incarnational body of Gautama. For a very helpful account of Steiner's use of this term by Robert McDermott see the American translation of these lectures, *According to Luke*, Anthroposophic Press, Great Barrington, MA 2001.
16. The Presentation in the Temple, Luke 2:25–35. Simeon was a reincarnation of Asita who did not live to see the Bodhisattva become a Buddha. See *The Gospel of St Luke*, lecture 2.
17. See Introduction and note 5.
18. See note 11.
19. Lecture, Berlin 14 November 1911, in *The Spiritual Hierarchies and the Physical World. Reality and Illusion/The Inner Realities of Evolution*, GA 132, Anthroposophic Press, Hudson, NY 1996/ Rudolf Steiner Publishing Co., London 1953.
20. See lecture 27 January 1908, in *Good and Evil Spirits/Influences of Spiritual Beings on Man*, GA 102, Rudolf Steiner Press, 2014/Anthroposophic Press, Hudson, NY 1982.
21. John R. Hinnells, *Persian Mythology*, Hamlyn, 1973.
22. *Bundahis*, Chap. 3:10–11, Sacred Books of the East, Vol. 5, 'Pahlavi Texts', Motilal Banarsidass, Delhi 1987.
23. *Zend-Avesta: Vendidad, Fargand 1 3(5)*, Sacred Books of the East, Vol. 4, Motilal Banarsidass, Delhi 1980.
24. In spiritual science the evolutionary stages of the earth's development. See note 11.
25. This is the more usual spelling in English—in the German original it is rendered Angro Mainyush. See note at the beginning regarding the name Ahura Mazda.
26. Rudolf Steiner Press, Sussex 1991.
27. See note 11 and for further references to earlier periods.

28. A term in use in the Theosophical Society to denote the second Person of the Trinity—the Son or Christ.
29. Details of Roncelin de Fos are taken from two articles by Jean-Pierre Schmit and Jean de Lauris in *Le Médiéviste Magazine*, Nr. 15 (Figeac, n.d.), no longer published.
30. Rainer Maria Rilke: *The Notebooks of Malte Laurids Brigge*, translated by Stephen Mitchell, Random House: Vintage International, 1990.
31. in *Good and Evil Spirits*, see note 20.
32. Emil Bock, *Kings and Prophets*, Chapter 27, Floris Books, Edinburgh 1989.
33. Hans Gsänger, 'Zaratas', *Mercury Star Journal*, Vol. V no. 3, Michaelmas 1979, translated from *Das Goetheanum*, Vol. 51, 1972.
34. Supplementary remarks—see above, plus further notes on the chronology of these events by the translator, Robert Powell, who suggests 'Darius' may really be Cyrus.
35. See note 32.
36. Rudolf Steiner, *From the History and Contents of the First Section of the Esoteric School 1904–1914*, GA 264, Part 1, Esoteric Lesson possibly held in Karlsruhe, 21 or 23 January 1911, Anthroposophic Press, Hudson, NY 1998.
37. Typescript K1, Rudolf Steiner House Library, London.
38. *Gnosis, the Mysteries and Christianity*, note 2, p. 38, Floris Books, Edinburgh 1994.
39. *Christianity as Mystical Fact and the Mysteries of Antiquity*, GA/CW 8, SteinerBooks, Great Barrington, MA 2006.
40. See R. Alan Culpepper, *John, the Son of Zebedee. The Life of a Legend*, T. & T. Clark, Edinburgh 2000. See especially note 32 on p. 87.
41. *Esoteric Christianity*, GA 130, Rudolf Steiner Press, 2000. For a summary of Lazarus-John's incarnations, see Margaret Jonas, *The Templar Spirit*, 'St John the Evangelist', Temple Lodge, 2011.

42. *The Catacombs. Pictures from the Life of Early Christianity*, edited and enlarged by Alfred Heidenreich from *Die Katakomben* by Emil Bock and Robert Goebel, The Christian Community Press, London 1962.
43. The Zarathustra ego entered the other Jesus' sheaths at age twelve. After 18 years he reached 30 when his ego withdrew to allow the Christ to enter fully into his sheaths.
44. The architect of King Solomon's temple. See Rudolf Steiner, *The Temple Legend*, GA 93, Rudolf Steiner Press, 1997.
45. For further on these themes, see lectures: Munich, 31 August 1909, in *The East in the Light of the West*, GA 113, Spiritual Science Library, Blauvelt, NY 1986; Berlin, 11 November 1904, *The Temple Legend*, GA 93 (see note 44); Berlin, 19 April 1917, in *Building Stones for an Understanding of the Mystery of Golgotha* (see note 4).
46. See note 35.
47. Lesson of Berlin, 22 October 1906, *Esoteric Lessons, Vol. 1*, GA 266/1, SteinerBooks, Great Barrington, MA 2007.
48. Düsseldorf, 5 May 1912, *The Festivals and Their Meaning: Easter*, GA 130, Rudolf Steiner Press, 1996.